T0381131

Snapshots

Kaye Brown

BALBOA.PRESS
A DIVISION OF HAY HOUSE

Balboa Press books may be ordered through booksellers or by contacting:

Balboa Press
A Division of Hay House
1663 Liberty Drive
Bloomington, IN 47403
www.balboapress.com
844-682-1282

Because of the dynamic nature of the Internet, any web addresses or links contained in this book may have changed since publication and may no longer be valid. The views expressed in this work are solely those of the author and do not necessarily reflect the views of the publisher, and the publisher hereby disclaims any responsibility for them.

The author of this book does not dispense medical advice or prescribe the use of any technique as a form of treatment for physical, emotional, or medical problems without the advice of a physician, either directly or indirectly. The intent of the author is only to offer information of a general nature to help you in your quest for emotional and spiritual well-being. In the event you use any of the information in this book for yourself, which is your constitutional right, the author and the publisher assume no responsibility for your actions.

Any people depicted in stock imagery provided by Getty Images are models, and such images are being used for illustrative purposes only. Certain stock imagery © Getty Images.

Print information available on the last page.

ISBN: 979-8-7652-5348-9 (sc)
ISBN: 979-8-7652-5347-2 (e)

Library of Congress Control Number: 2024917747

Balboa Press rev. date 08/30/2024

Foreword

Our journey in this realm called Life is dictated by many definitions, both personal and inference. Our main aim is personal, which sometimes can be culturally bound after which we begin our progression to inference.

Choosing many times from options, all of which may be less than attractive, tests our resilience along with strengthening our mettle. Even as steel must be heated to create strength, we expose ourselves to extremes of vibrational energy equivalent to the heat or energy used to strengthen steel. We do this in our quest to affirm or negate our beliefs and deservedness, or lack thereof. Outside forces or energy clarifies our beliefs causing decisions and actions based on said beliefs, thus creating the reality in which we live. Our emotions are the indicator of whether we are honoring ourselves or denying ourselves. They are not an indicator of the rightness or wrongness of anything other than us looking to create a reality we can be comfortable residing in.

Emotions such as frustration, indignation, resentment, and envy or whatever negative emotion we are experiencing and seeking solace for is telling us we are not living the existence we were created to inhabit and the changes we are charged with making live within not without. Courage is the antidote for stopping the blame cycle we so often engage in by trying to attribute our shortcomings to things other than ourselves. All this is needed for us to face and encompass our emotions as simply a feeling, creating an outside force, creating an inner belief that a thing is true or not. With this mindset I proceed. Everything reported in these writings is true for me, with the understanding of truth being unique to the individual and not absolute. Personal truth is colored by beliefs which are filtered through Life experience.

Thoughts of lower density (negativity) cause us to expose ourselves to matching energy creating in our environment matching results of forecasted events. Higher density (positivity) thoughts allow us to realize the power of possibility. We must create words and actions to bring about better content to our days thus bringing a better Life experience.

Challenges are personal and not especially hard, except for how we perceive them. Softening our thought, we can conjure a better scenario to entice a more positive unfolding. Until then, we must keep repeating our behavior.

This creation is garnered from my personal life experience. One of maintenance of our individuality, rather than adhering to unproductive practices simply because of cultural training. Belonging first to oneself with adherence to the spirit leading to honest open dialogue.

Part One ————————

This story begins on the day of my birth, December 8, 1953. My earliest memory is being around two years old, sitting in a highchair. It's suppertime. We are eating beans and cornbread. Only wanting the soup with no beans in it, I had found a bean and was throwing a fit. Mama came, took my bowl, removed the bean and all was well.

Up to this point in my existence I had been able to be a child and the "hard times" so familiar to my family had not been visited on me. By "hard times" I am referring to starvation. This memory would visit me many times throughout my childhood when we were without necessities. I believe this is where my feelings of guilt began. Self-chastisement for exhibiting a need for choice when I should have been thankful just to be able to eat. Another requirement at this time was wanting the crust torn off bread, when we had store bought bread. As a child I could in no way realize this was a natural development to display preferences. Displaying preferences did not bode well in the environment of the culture in which I was born into. Somehow in later years when hard times visited, I felt had I not been so "picky" we wouldn't have to be going through the things we were experiencing.

The area of the country where I was born is a community called Spring Creek, Arkansas located in Lee County. My father said it was so called because there was a branch (creek) running through there where people would come get their water because it was spring fed. I don't know if this is true or not. My father had a story about most things. I loved his stories and believed them, especially the one about where I came from. He and mama were walking in the garden one fine day and heard a sound like a kitten mewing. Moving a cabbage leaf aside there I was just lying there in the dirt. Never questioning him about the particulars of the story, since I was born in the winter, I would listen wide-eyed, amazed and in awe thankful they had decided to take a walk in the garden that day. My reasoning abilities remiss because I believed his story and knew I was special. Spring Creek is still a rural area, but in 1953 it was an area of extreme poverty. There was no way to make a living unless one left the area which at the time of the beginning of my story my brother Zack had done. Taking the role of breadwinner for our family he had gone to Little Rock to secure employment. This was how we were able to eat.

On the day of my birth the place we called home was really a shack of two rooms. A front room with beds and a kitchen. The kitchen had a wood cook stove, but the house was drafty and on cold days it was impossible to warm.

Mama would have the younger kids leave the house when the time for birthing came. My sister Lucy was fifteen at the time, so while Daddy went to get the doctor she stayed with Mama. I decided to come before Daddy got back with the doctor, so Lucy, who unbeknownst to the rest of the family was pregnant herself, delivered me, under Mama's direction. This had to be a traumatic experience for her.

Mama could not decide what to name me, so the doctor simply put female child and the required information on whatever form they used to send the information of a live birth. She had two names she liked. One was naming me after Daddys niece Miranda and the other one is the one I wound up with, named after her mother who had died in the flu epidemic of 1918. Took her two weeks to decide so it turned out I had no name registered until 2002 when I mailed the capitol for a birth certificate copy and was instructed to take a person older than me who could swear to my identity to a notary and return proof before a birth certificate could be issued, which is what I did.

Nineteen fifty-six or thereabout is my second recollection. I'm standing behind the heating stove in the front room. It was winter and hard times were on us. Two of my older sisters had gone out with a grass sack. It was a burlap bag, but we called it a grass sack. They had caught a possum and had it in the sack. To me they seemed grown, but they were children of ten or twelve years of age. It was Joyce and Rose who were doing the deed. Placing the poker across the neck of the possum, standing on either end of it they were pulling on its tail to break its neck. We then would boil and eat it. Unsuccessful in their attempts, Daddy stepped in and finished the job. We ate it because that was all we had to eat. I found out at an early age I did not like possum. How we managed to survive that winter I do not know but we did. Perhaps there was some outside intervention. My younger brother would have been a year or two old at the time. Mother would have become pregnant with my youngest brother during this period. There was a whole gang of us, fifteen to be exact, fourteen live births and one stillborn. Mama always said she had two families since the age difference was so great between us. She began having babies soon after marriage and continued about every two years until the last one. My baby brother was the only one she went to the hospital to birth, and she was told if she had any more, she wouldn't make it, so she and daddy stopped sleeping together.

My next memory, I'm sitting on an old wooden table constructed of planks nailed onto two by fours, pushed up against the side of the house. The house is a log cabin consisting of a big room with a lean-to attached. Grandfather Mamas daddy had already passed away, so we had moved from the place I was born into this place. We called it down in the holler, still do when we speak about it, reason being it was down a seemingly, in recollection big hill. Probably was not that big but I'm four years old so it seemed big to me.

Since I'm only four years old I fail to understand what is going on in our family. All I know is Mama is in bed with the baby (brother Reginald) and Daddy is sad, worried, or depressed. Probably all three. My two sisters who were the oldest ones at home at that time had run away. Joyce and Rose were the ones who had decided something needed to happen because of the dire circumstances we were having. They had walked to Lucys house some twenty miles away, to try to get some help for us.

Baby Reginald was starving. Mama's milk had dried up because of lack of nutrition. All she was able to give him was apple juice and reconstituted dried milk we got from commodities. Recollection of this time is colored by conversations garnered from older siblings whose remembering is more concise than my four-year-old memory. My memory is more of a feeling of wanting Mama and Daddy to be happy and knowing something was wrong.

Sitting on the table I watched a lizard flitting between the logs. In and out in and out. Climbing down I went to Mama who was lying in bed in the front room. She patted my cheek and told me to get a spoon off the table and bring her one of those yellow apples we had, so I did. She took the spoon and began scraping pulp from the apple and taking a bite and giving me a bite. This memory is clear to me. It could be fabrication, but it makes me feel good to think about it. She had to have cut the apple in half because in my memory it was cut in half. There was an orchard on the farm planted by Grandfather.

Lucys husband worked at public work so I supposed Joyce and Rose figured they could help us. By this time, they had a family, and times were hard for everyone so I'm sure they didn't have anything to spare.

With no communication with the outside world other than writing a letter, which required a postage stamp which cost money which we had none of, or walking which required food for strength, saying we were in a crisis would be putting it mildly.

Recollecting this time with an older sister, she thinks it is springtime, which makes sense because Reginald was born in May. She recalls Daddy cooking supper which according to her was fried green tomatoes breaded with the last of the cornmeal. She said we had two apiece. Joyce and Rose had left for fear the baby would starve to death. By this time, they were nearing their teen years and felt something must be done I'm certain.

Father ruled the household with an iron fist, uncompromising, so there was no way Joyce and Rose could have voiced their fears surrounding the circumstance we were in. Our household, being cultish in nature, with a strong patriarchal presence, Mother was a quiet presence, never going against Father at all. Accepting her lot in life because of the love she had for her children and my father. Modeling herself as a Christian with the bible being her directive, she attempted making the best of the situation in which she found herself. The bible was the only book allowed in the house for years. They were united in the presentation of what a couple needed to be, never harboring resentment toward one another, with the biggest problem being eating regularly. This period was a challenging time for all of us. Seemingly hopeless yet hope remained.

Daddy had been working with my oldest sisters' husband Smith Dankworth, in junk cars. Smith always fooled with car parts and things of that nature, stripping copper, and selling it for a little money. Working public work was frowned on, suggesting one was incapable of being capable. Capable 0f what I don't know. He had just gotten home and was in the barn. Cheryl, who was twelve years old at the time, recalls she had gotten home from school and went inside the cabin to check on Mama and the baby. "How's the baby?" she asked. "He's there" Mama said, gesturing toward the bed where Reginald lay. Cheryl picked him up. He was breathing but too weak to cry. Putting him back on the bed, she went to the barn to see Daddy. "How's the baby" he asked? She replied, "he's dying, not good.". Daddy became angry, snarling at her, "you young'uns liable to say anything". "The older ones said he was fine". Going into the house he saw Mama sitting in the same spot she was in when Cheryl had come home from school.

"Ezra, we've got to do something here", Mama told him. Picking up the lifeless body of his last born he along with Mama walked the path through the woods to Sister and Smith's house. Smith had a car, so he drove them to Lee County hospital in Marianna. Upon arrival they began feeding Reginald intravenously. Afterward, when Mama related this story to us, she said the doctor told her another day and he would have been dead, from starvation, in the United States of America in 1958.

To understand this, I cannot. I know the mindset attached. My research of poverty per Google states it is an idea that a thing is only happening to you personally and no one else experiences hardships. Personally, I believe the reason for our life being the way it was and having an instance such as the above-mentioned is an inability to take responsibility for one's own existence along with immaturity on the adults' role in the provision of family. This had been a way of life for my family all the way through. This is the only one I can recall. It's strange but I do not recall being hungry, all I recall is the pallor hanging over the household and knowing something was wrong because there was no happiness and wanting there to be.

Recollection of this incident causes consternation within even now all these years later. My inability to grasp why anyone would choose such an existence caused me to abhor love statements because I knew my parents loved us and yet allowing such an atrocity to happen proved to me that love was something to be feared because of the calamities it would make one endure. This perhaps is the reason I've been married five times and endured much abuse at the hands of ones professing to love and cherish me and I them. Sometimes kindness and love being manifested can be perceived as weakness, and the suffering and doing without we lived taught me love was a weakness to avoid it because of the pain it brought. It took me many years and much sorrow to dispel the negative mindset this teaching wrought.

My family moved from the cabin to a shanty at the top of the hill from down in the holler. This place was owned by a man by the name of Joe Cotton. He and his wife owned a country store. It was up the dirt road from where we moved to. This was where we got groceries when we had any money. They would allow people to run a ticket and get things on credit until they got money from whatever source of income they may have. Since Father seldom held gainful employment, we could get things rarely.

After moving to the top of the hill things seemingly got better for us. Daddy and brother Zack got a job at the box factory in neighboring Monroe County. Smith got a job there as well. Since he had a car, they had transportation and rode together. Knowing the car they had was on its last leg, they decided to pool resources and buy a better one to ensure they had reliable transportation. The plan was to share this vehicle. My brother Zack had a driver's license so one weekend he would keep the car and the next weekend Smith would keep it. My Father never drove, nor owned a car. Initially, this arrangement worked well until it didn't.

There was a bar on the County line. This place cashed peoples' paychecks on Friday which was payday. Daddy and Zack loved to drink. Smith, as I recall, never drank much. As most weaknesses of character can be preyed on by others, Smith used this as he was predatory by nature, which at that time, as now, is true of us all. Denying this fact is a denial of the learning process of living.

They began buying beer and whiskey sometimes when they cashed their paychecks. I can recall good times of Mama and Daddy having what she called a hot toddy which was whiskey, sugar and hot water mixed. Sometimes she would let me have a taste. Even though we did not have electricity, Daddy would hook a battery-operated radio up to a car battery and we would listen to the Grand Ole Opry on Friday and Saturday nights. Mama and Daddy would dance and all us kids that were still at home would sit lined up on the bed listening and loving the camaraderie of a good time. Smith never came in the house when it was his turn to keep the car, he just dropped them off. When it was our turn to keep the car, they dropped him off at the place where he and my oldest sister Vera lived.

One Friday I recall Mother saying, "I hope they don't stop at bar today." But they did. I'm sure she and Daddy had been having conversations about things that had occurred in the past. Things I as a child had only an inkling of, only hearing snippets of words and stuff from older siblings, and not knowledge of life as it was, only wanting my family and everyone in it to be happy. She was worried because she knew my father's way of thinking. His animalistic nature when crossed and the egotistic adhesion of the pursuit of righting perceived wrongs rather than acceptance of what another presented and if the behavior is unacceptable, changing contact with that person by putting them out of one's life rather than dwelling on misdeeds. Dependency causes this type of mentality. At that time, people had to depend on one another. Opportunity for self-sufficiency was scarce and this person was married into the family.

Earlier in the week Smith had informed Daddy that he wanted to keep the car on the weekend coming up and it was not his turn. The inability to express his thoughts or a mindset of thinking someone was "stepping on his toes" caused Father to agree, yet rumination began on the agreement and anger took over. Anticipation of a showdown ensued. He knew what he was planning but true to his nature he involved others so if the plan failed, he had someone to blame. He had already told Mama what he had planned. Zack knew as well. They did not want the plan to manifest yet it did cause my mother to worry, knowing something was going to happen and it would not be pretty.

"Stay here in the car", Daddy told Zack, "I've got something in the house I want to give Smith." The tension was palpable. Zack stayed put in the backseat though, everyone always obeyed Father or paid the price of not. Smith was nobody's fool even though he was many other things. He knew he had crossed lines no one should ever cross and live to tell the tale. He remained in the driver's seat, with the car still running. The energy in the car had been brewing but had escalated after stopping at the bar. My Father was a violent man and was repulsed by the display of what he perceived as disrespect by changing the agreement of car sharing. Rigid in thinking and harboring resentment that had been stewing for years he was angry. Very angry. The anger he felt was obvious from the energy he was exuding.

Zack remained in the backseat, sipping on his beer. The rest of the beer was on the floorboard at his feet. The unease of both Smith and Zack prevented them from having any conversation, just sitting there waiting for Daddy to come back. Silence was tension so strong it could be felt and Smith all at once had an epiphany. "Get out of this car", he said. Zack was reluctant to do so because of what Daddy had said. He didn't say a word, just remained sitting there. Smith's heart was pounding, and he began to sweat. "I said get out of this car right now or you're going with me, that old man is going to blow my head off". About that time Daddy emerged out the door shotgun in hand. Being a four-door car Zack just had time to exit before Smith squealed out of the dirt yard, dust flying and Oertals 92 beer cans flying everywhere. The tumult was over for Smith but had only begun for us.

Daddy was in a rage and determined to release it on someone, and we were the only ones there so that is where it became directed. At first it was Zack, "why did you let that son of a bitch leave?" he roared. Knowing better than to reply with any answer because there was no answer to suffice, he simply made no reply. He knew what was coming his way, so he took the beating he knew he had coming. Not defending himself, he allowed Father to beat him mercilessly. All of us kids were scared to death. Mama knew the rage had to be spent and there was nothing she could do. All five of us kids who were still at home, were out in the yard watching this, scared and crying. Finally, Daddy wore himself out or came to his senses and realized what he was doing, either way he finally stopped. I can still see in my mind's eye the brother I loved so much, shirt in shreds, bloody face and clothes walk past all us kids going in the house and going to bed.

Zack not obeying Daddy was not the reason for this happening. It was a much deeper emotional upheaval of suppression of himself. A much deeper and darker reality not being dealt with along with an attempt to forgive and move forward all the while seeing that his forgiveness was being interpreted as weakness of character and ignorance. This was the cause of the intense anger released onto my brother.

Unfortunately for Mama it was her turn next. Daddy had always favored Ezra Jr. over all of us. Ezra Jr. began jumping on a bed that was in the front room. It was positioned against the wall but had enough room between the wall for a small child to fall into, which is what he did. Mama went to tend to him, and Father rushed over, pushing her out of the way, he jerked the bed away from the wall and retrieved him. I cannot remember what happened next. Experiences of such violence observed by children can cause much mental anguish and adverse circumstances to ensue. This event was the end of employment for Daddy and Zack.

Smith Dankworth was a 21-year-old man when he married my oldest sister, Vera. My Father and he had been working on the railroad together and Daddy befriended him. Daddy brought him home to meet the family, so he surely had made a good impression at first. Vera was of "marrying age", maybe a few years past because she was seventeen at the time. Mama had been fourteen when she and Daddy married, and years later she told me she really was thirteen. Once a girl turned twenty-one, she was considered an old maid. My Father believed women were for sexual gratification and childbearing and that was the extent of their reason for being. Finding someone to marry was the first thing to do rather than employment to take care of a family then making the family. The belief was the Lord would provide. Faith was the thing to have and if anyone professed wanting anything other than what they were told to do, and follow suit, were an outcast. Going as far as ridicule and ostracizing them, causing a feeling of shame and undeserving equal to isolation. People pleasing was taught and self-development frowned upon.

Smith was a short stocky man, dark haired and brown skinned. Swarthy is the word coming to mind when I think of him. He always had an odor about him of musty/motor oil. I was terrified of him. He would say things to me like, "do you like ice cream?" or "do you want some candy?" It embarrassed me so much I can remember my

11

face burning with embarrassment. In my recollection he was always in the family, and I always felt ill at ease around him. I always felt ill at ease around most of my family except for Mama.

As I said, the main objective for girls was marriage and having a family. Since we lived in such isolation it was difficult to meet anyone other than kinfolk and my father always talked about intermarriage and how it could cause many problems genetically. Of course, he didn't use that term, I'm sure he had never heard that term since he only had a fourth-grade education, he said. Mama had taught him to write his name, but he couldn't read or write anything other than that. He was embarrassed by this, and I could feel it even as a small child. Getting the girls married off was an objective of him and Mama too since she went along with him on most things, especially at that time. So, during these years they felt a girl needed to be married between the ages of fourteen to sixteen years of age. If they were not my father would go on rants, calling them names and blaming Mama for only having girls, even though the male determines the sex of a child. He didn't know this or else he just wanted to blame someone for his lot in life rather than seeking to change it. I'm relating this not because it was spoken because as a belief, it wasn't, rather it was implied that women were less than men even from birth.

The patriarchal environment in which I was raised caused me to defer to men my whole life, accepting behavior from them causing much consternation all the way from mistaking abusive words as love to subjecting myself and consequently my children to situations of utter terror and fear for our life. All in the name of love.

Since there were so many children in the family, mostly girls, Smith Dankworth saw them as "fodder" for his sexual appetite. No judgement here, simply the fact of the matter that was common knowledge in the family, and this was the unresolved rage driving my father's behavior in this snapshot memory of mine. There was never a fair hearing of any occurrence of how I or my sisters might be feeling about anything, especially where my brother Ezra Jr. was concerned. Accepting this as the way of things never bothered me. It was always whatever my father said right or wrong because anything other than that would cause him to behave in ways none of us wanted to experience.

One statement Father made stands out in my mind that shaped my thinking concerning love was when I was around ten years old. Hard times were on us, and we were out of school on Christmas break. We kids could eat at school, but we had maybe two weeks off. Mama had used the last of the flour to make biscuits with one morning. While we are eating, she said in a matter-of-fact way, "Ezra, that's the last of the flour." I became scared inside because I feared what lay ahead. She kept the meal and flour in five-gallon containers, having lids that seated onto the canister bottom, made from metal (tin) that we had bought lard in. These containers kept the mice from getting in there. Going into the kitchen I looked in the flour container. It was empty. I recalled my selfishness of wanting the crust torn off bread and wished I had those crusts then.

We had gone several days without food, and we stayed in bed, to conserve energy I guess, I don't really know. By this time after all the years of suffering, listening to Father explain his way of thinking concerning family and what it meant to him he began to speak, 'we may starve to death, but at least we will be together, we'll starve together in a pile," at least we love each other." Mama spoke up, "this isn't right, people aren't supposed to live like this, you need to go make a raid". It escalated from there. No one was allowed to attempt to dissuade his way of being. Even Mama going against him scared me. She wouldn't back down and I began to feel sorry for him. Her tirade was so strong. I do not recall how long it lasted but I do recall her saying, "you get out that door and don't come back here until you have some food for these kids to eat." It took much courage for her to do this, and as he went out the door, she heaved a stick of stove wood at him, hitting the inside of the door as he left. My takeaway from all this was never love anyone because it caused people to suffer and do without.

I'm sure there were people in the area where we lived who were aware of our circumstances. We had some neighbors living down the hill from us. They always killed a hog every year. They were country people who knew how to get by. It seemed as if we didn't know how to get by. The man had been a blacksmith in his younger days, and they still went to town in a wagon drawn by mules. I suppose they were on social security at the time. Mama sent myself and my two older sisters down to their house to ask for some food. They gave us some meat from their smokehouse and probably some flour and meal. All I really remember was the meat though. Going back to the house I think Daddy was back by that time. Mama or Susan, who was the oldest one home at the time began to cook what they had given us. We were so happy to get something to eat and yet Daddy continued to portray his depressed attitude and refused to eat. Associating love with suffering and doing without it became clear to me that to love another one must deprive oneself. Daddy had money in his pocket at the time. One hundred dollars to be exact, garnered from the selling a calf Uncle Alna his brother had given him to care for and sell for him. I think he did this because he always worked away from home and couldn't take care of it. Uncle Alna was supposed to come get the money once the calf was sold. Mama thought he needed to take the money and buy groceries with it, but Daddy felt otherwise. That was the reason she threw the stick of wood at him. When he returned, he had bought some groceries, and had probably eaten as well. That is why he wouldn't eat what we had gotten from the neighbors. His goal was to make us feel sorry for him. It worked. Seemed he was forever attempting to cause us to feel bad or unhappy by manipulation of our emotions.

Either way it always worked for me because I always responded to his output of emotion. Not teaching personal self-regulation, the goal if there was one was to dampen the spirit of happiness displayed even if it meant starving everyone down to dampen our spirits. This is how I interpreted it. What is closer to the truth is my parents were overwhelmed, uneducated, carrying the effects of past life hardship along with an inability to accept and deal effectively with the reality they had created. Children lack the capacity of life experience to know and process anything other than what they need and want.

School years were in many ways a blessing even though they brought home many painful truths. As a child it is hard to experience the atrocities associated with going without breakfast and being thought of as being sick when before lunch at times, I didn't feel like holding my head up and would lay it down on the desk. After lunch I would feel so much better. My teachers obviously didn't know how to recognize childhood hunger. Starting out in grade one though I could already read because my sister, two years my elder had taught me from the books she brought home. I knew my ABCs and could count to one hundred. Other children could not read as well, so wanting to fit in I copied their behavior and stumbled and paused over the words the same way they did.

Being away from Mama was the hardest part. I would never cry at school but began as soon as I got home. It was a truly grieving process I was going through.

We still lived in the house down the dirt road from the store. We had to walk a good way up the dirt road to the store where the bus stop was. Starting my first year in 1960 because of my birthday being in December, I turned seven in grade one. Not really knowing we were that much different than others I thought nothing of going barefoot to school until getting there and seeing everyone else wearing shoes. Upon this observation I recall trying to hide my feet which was impossible, so I just put one foot on top of the other one. Never would I dream of letting my parents know how I felt because I was forever looking out for their feelings and wanting them to be happy. We were all geared that way, to think of others before ourselves.

The school was the biggest building I had ever been in. Three stories high, with the first floor being elementary grades one through eight, and second floor high school, nine through twelve. The lunchroom was in the basement. Lunch cost a quarter, but we always got free lunch, and when we went through the lunch line every day the lady collecting the quarter made us say free. Right in front of everybody it was humiliating even for a child. They had to be getting some kind of perverse pleasure from making us say that.

Eating lunch was a huge motivator to go to school though. The aroma emanating from the lunchroom was intoxicating. There was nothing they served I didn't like. They made homecooked food such as meatloaf, mashed potatoes, and the milk was in little glass half pint bottles, so cold and delicious. I wouldn't drink milk at home because when we had a cow, we didn't have refrigeration, so the milk was warm, and I just didn't like it. Extra servings of milk could be bought for a penny, but we never had an extra cent to get one. I could have eaten many more servings than we got but believe me I thoroughly enjoyed the meal I got and was thankful for it. I'm amazed that any of us done as well academically as we did. Forever the worrier, I would think about Mama and Daddy, and wish they could have the lunches we had.

One day in grade three my teacher thought I was sick because I had my head lying on my desk. She told me I wasn't getting enough sunshine and made me go outside and sit in the sun. I was so weak from hunger, along with sitting in the sun made it worse and I began sweating profusely. This was before lunch. After lunch I was fine. Sometimes she would be good to me and other times she would say things I knew were directed at me. Learning came easy for me in the elementary school years, especially having the support of my older sister being one year ahead of me helping me grasp the things we were studying. She would take me out in the dirt yard, take a stick and teach me how to do whatever the teacher had told us we were going to be working on the next day. Always the worrier, I thought we were supposed to know how to do it, not that they were going to teach us. I would tell her, "The teacher said we are going to start division tomorrow", she would say "don't worry, I'll teach you tonight". I depended on her so much.

Workbooks cost ten cents and we were never able to get them when needed so my teacher would sit me beside someone who had a workbook, and I would copy onto my paper whatever we were working on. Observing other children scribbling on a clean sheet of paper, then throwing it away, I would wait until I thought no one was looking maybe at recess or another time when I could find the opportunity, and trying to be unobtrusive, I would retrieve the paper and use the clean side to do my schoolwork. In this manner was how I was able to get my needs met as far as possible. We were never able to purchase our school pictures when the time came. One time in particular my sister Joyce, who was babysitting for a couple who lived in the city rode the greyhound bus home for a visit. Riding the bus was the manner of transportation at the time. Even though she only made fifteen dollars a week, she managed to save money and was forever trying to make things better for us kids. Doing special things for us other than pure survival. I don't know how much the pictures cost, but she bought them for us. I was so proud and happy to be able to exchange pictures with the other children and participate in what seemingly everyone else took for granted. When the teacher collected the money for the pictures, I felt such a part of everything until she stood before the class and announced how she couldn't believe how some people would choose to buy a child's school pictures and not buy them a ten-cent workbook. I knew she was talking to me even though she had not directed the statement to me. She definitely "rained on my parade" that day. It is still hard for me to understand the motivation behind the commentary. It really hurt my feelings and wiped out the happiness I had felt. I know I wasn't the only one in my school doing without things I needed, but that's how it seemed to me. The nature of children it seemed was to ridicule and pick on the less fortunate. They, for some reason, were never as mean to me as they were to others. One day in the school yard at recess a little boy saw a discarded half of an ice cream, he picked it up and ate it, and the group of children who participated in the ridiculing began to say mean things to him. He was terribly embarrassed, and I felt so bad for him. If I had it to do over again, I would defend him, but I was just glad they weren't bullying me. To this day, even though I now know no one gets through life without sorrow and grief, I still have ill feelings toward the people perpetrating the actions I observed that day. They did this in front of me and I wonder what their motive could have been. Even to this day I must say it feels bad to me to think about it. Not speaking up for him, and asking the bullies to stop, but I didn't know how to do that because I'd never been taught. The teachers didn't speak up for them either and they were there and heard as well what was going on. Perhaps they had not been schooled themselves in dealing with bullies, but the things I experienced from my teacher was adverse behavior, so forgiveness is in order, I guess. All in all, though I had kind and caring teachers some of whom went above and beyond to assist me in my development.

My fourth-grade teacher Mrs. Eddison is one worthy of mention as well as my sixth and eighth-grade teachers. Mrs. Eddison knew my situation of poverty and one year she and Mrs. Harrison, the eighth-grade teacher, got together and took me and my sister shopping for winter coats and shoes. I don't know where they got the money, if it was theirs or maybe they knew about some program of assistance but wherever it came from it was a good thing and I am so grateful.

My sixth-grade teacher was a man. He was young, perhaps twenty-three or four years old at the time. He approached teaching in a way that my previous teachers had not. It seemed he attempted to cultivate a more creative side in the children. We would listen to classical music, close our eyes and simply let our mind connect with our hands and freely scribble to the sound of the music. There was no right or wrong way to do it and it was not graded. This seemed to level the playing field between the students who were more academically accomplished and those who came to school just because their parents sent them. One project he suggested I do if I could keep up with my regular classwork was draw the eagle on the back of the dollar bill. Each day I was allowed to go downstairs to the lunchroom after lunch was over and use what I think was drafting paper, because it was big, and on a roll, and draw the picture of the eagle. Using a lead pencil to draw it, then using colored pencils to color it in with. Once it was finished, he posted it on the bulletin board in the entry hall across from the principals' office. It was a project I took very seriously and thought of as a job. Never once though did I feel special because of it. I thought it was something that needed to be done and I was the one who could do it. He stands out as one of the best if not the best teachers I ever had. Seeing a man take interest and being encouraging was something I wasn't used to. The standards set in my home environment were authoritarian and male dominated so anything else was strange to me. This thinking has colored my relationship with the male species throughout my life in a detrimental way. Never feeling accepted nor loved by my father, his harshness caused me to second guess myself by being harsh and judgmental with myself along with an unforgiveness of myself for any perceived infraction on my part and allowing any behavior on the part of any partner I had at the time to go unchecked. All the while allowing near constant chastisement from them, reflected my emotional relationship with my father. Even my immediate family members' criticism could elicit within myself an attempt to please them other than myself, coloring my thoughts still.

Mrs. Harrison, my eighth-grade teacher, had a reputation for being mean from the talk I'd heard from my older sisters. At least that is how I integrated it into my thinking. She would present as gruff, but she was a sweetheart. She would talk to us about washing our bodies and clothes and tell us as a class there was no excuse to not be clean. No matter what she said, "you all have access to soap and water". She made extra effort to encourage me. I don't know if she was that way with the others, but she was with me. There was a statewide competition for eighth grade students to write a soil conservation essay. Each school in the county would choose the best from their eighth-grade class and submit them for evaluation to determine the winner. The competition in our class came down to two entries. Another classmate and I were the finalists. Unsure of the judges or what criteria was used, it was announced that I had won. The winners from all the county schools were given a dinner at the high school which was several miles from Spring Creek. With no manner of transportation, she told me not to worry about it, she would come pick me up and take me if I met her at the home of a friend of mine who lived on the main road. I was nervous, but excited at the same time. She felt the same way, I'm sure. It was out of her way and required extra effort on her part because she lived in a neighboring town. She came and got me, we attended the dinner and then she took me back to my friend's house. All this driving amounts to about fifty miles probably and she wasn't a young woman and had a life of her own. We had a steak dinner there at the high school. She cut my steak up for me and fixed my baked potato by slitting it, squeezing it from both ends and putting butter in the split. I still till this day do my potatoes like that. So much effort was put into me by those teachers. I am so grateful for them. I'm sure when they heard about what happened in my life at the hands of my family, they were disappointed and somewhat angry.

My experience of the male and female roles in family life were conflicted with the things observed outside my home. In my home the message takeaway of a man was one an authoritative all-knowing individual to be feared along with accepting any behavior displayed, weather it was right or wrong. My parents never once complimented me on my academic abilities, nor did they ever look at my report card when it was brought home, I signed it myself. Other children would talk about their parents giving them a quarter for every A they got on their report card, and I felt different because I had to sign my own and my parents never looked at it. I felt grateful they had allowed me to attend the ceremony for the essay contest. Never feeling sorry for myself, I do not think any of my teachers felt sorry for me, they were simply encouraging and doing all they could to assist me. My feelings were more of the nature of feeling I could compete in the arena of learning, even though I may not have the other things my peers had, I could use my mind to make good grades and excel in that manner. I must say the teachers I had in my life at the time probably knew more about my situation than I was aware of. Some of them had taught my older siblings so they were cognitive of the stamina involved in making the effort to be involved in learning.

High school was not a good experience for me, even though I had gone to summer school to learn my way around the building at Mrs. Harrisons' suggestion. The county schools had consolidated, and the high school was large enough to accommodate that. Summer school went well, but when the school year started it seemed, I could not acclimate to the environment. The teachers were not of the same caliber I had gotten used to. Now it is clear they were just doing a job and not truly interested in the success of the students. One teacher, my science teacher, had no control of the classroom at all. He would leave the book of the test he was going to give us lying on his desk and allow a student who was in the class to access it and get the answers. This student would then pass the answers around to all of us with instruction not to get all the answers correct, but we all made a passing grade. This lack of care along with the personal things I was dealing with culminated in a real lack of interest on my part. Along with this was my ineptness in communicating my needs to anyone, I began feeling like I did in my own home, unseen, unheard, and not considered at all. Perhaps because it was the onset of teenage years, I don't know. There had been many changes that had taken place at home so that had some bearing on it as well. Sister Mary who was two years older than me, had gotten married to a man named Jack Bannon. She was sixteen and he was twenty-four years old. His parents had owned the place where we lived at the time. It wasn't much of a house, having three large rooms and three porches, a front porch and two screened in porches on either side of the kitchen. Still no indoor plumbing, it was a better place than where we had been living. Calling it the red house because it had red siding on it. After they got married, I was the oldest one at home and it weighed heavily on my mentality. The oldest child had many responsibilities to fulfil. Washing the clothes and cleaning the house on the weekend in addition to any school assignments left little time for anything else.

Mary moved in with Jack and his family. His mother had breast cancer and it had gone to her brain, so she had become bedridden. Mary became her caretaker along with running the household and going to high school. Without Mary to lean on and be a friend I was somewhat adrift unknown to my parents or even myself, I took my role as housekeeping very seriously.

We moved from the red house to a community called Turkey Scratch. Mama and Daddy had bought the place. It was awful. No well, we had to drink pond water that Mama would boil and put chlorine in to make it clean enough to drink. The house had two rooms, with no privacy at all. Even though the rooms were large there was no way to have a place to get away from the others. There were five of us living there. It was difficult to clean myself and my clothes, so I was presentable for school. Along with all this was the financial problem of having to buy schoolbooks. In elementary school the books had been furnished but high school was different. Since Mary was a grade ahead of me, I could use some of her books, but some of the books were changed from the previous year and had to be bought new. Worry was my constant companion and I felt I had no one to share with after Mary left.

I got through and passed my freshman year and began my sophomore year. My memory of that year is near nonexistent. Living in this new community, the best part if there was one was, we didn't have to walk to catch the bus and stand out in the cold. About all I recall of my sophomore year is dropping out halfway through and following in the steps of the path most of my sisters had taken. The ones who had not taken the path were labeled by my father with derogatory names and I did not want that to happen to me.

Blame defined by Merriam Webster dictionary is to find fault with, to hold responsible, at fault. Placing blame is counterproductive in my opinion. Personally, the unfolding of events up to and including my dropping out of school is dictated more by observation and my perception of my culture and the expectations of said culture more than anything else. Speaking with Mary about these events years later she said all I needed to do was ask Daddy for whatever I needed, and he would take care of it. There is no way for me to know if this is true or not. Mary did tend to wear rose colored glasses where our family was concerned. As for myself, I learned that no matter the need it would not be filled. I think I formed this notion when I looked in the empty flour bin years earlier. My takeaway was if there was a need, you had to look to yourself to fill it.

Our neighbors where we moved, was a family by the name of Jones. There was a girl in the family a few years younger than me, and we became fast friends. I had never had a friend live so nearby. We visited each other daily and would walk to the neighborhood store together when we had money. She seemed more knowledgeable about things than I. Life In general for me had always been focused on lack and need. Just hanging out and taking walks, giggling and laughing were somewhat foreign to me. This is what we did, just be kids and have fun.

Her mother had a car and could drive. They were good to me and included me when they could in any activities they could. One fall day in 1969 they invited me to go to the Monroe County fair with them. Asking Mama, she agreed that I could. Simple things such as this can have such an impact on one's life, changing its trajectory all the way around. We went to the fair. Walking through the fairgrounds, she spotted some boys leaning up against a car. She knew them and went over to talk. Introducing me to them, the older boy asked me for a date. I said I had never dated before, and I didn't know if my Daddy would let me. He said he would ask my Daddy if I could go to the drive in with him. This was on a Saturday. I said okay. The next day he came down to our house and talked with my dad, and the following Saturday I went to the drive in with him.

It was fun to be able to go places. Not that we went to that many places but going to the Tasty Freeze and having a burger and fries then seeing a movie at the drive in theater was a big deal to someone like me. I really didn't want to kiss and hug and pretend to be an adult because I still felt like a child. I always had to be home by nine o'clock and can remember this because when I got home, I'd watch The Carol Burnette show and it came on at nine o'clock.

Gary Edward Newman was the boy's name, but everyone called him Eddie. He was seventeen years old but thought he was grown. At fifteen I still felt like a child and just liked getting out of the house. It wasn't long before he took me to meet his parents. They were totally different than mine. They both worked at jobs. His dad was a county grader driver and his mom cleaned houses for people. They were much younger than my parents and the dynamics of the household were different. His being more matriarchal while my family was patriarchal.

Accepting me as their own, when he asked me to marry him it was crazy, and I knew it. No one else seemed to know it. He didn't have a job, had never had a job, with his mother paying for his car payment, his little sister and her husband living in the house with his mom and dad and that was where we were going to live.

He had given me a ring that looked like the prizes that come in Cracker Jack boxes. Only wearing it when we went on a date, I hid it from Mama and Daddy and never told them he had asked me to get married. It was totally embarrassing to me. This is how inexperience, immaturity and disconnection can alter the course of one's life. Simply going to a county fair caused an alteration in my existence and a reinforcement of the stacking of our societies gender order of importance. My grades began to decline in school and the fear of having to get married to a kid that didn't even have a job had taken over my whole thought process. Unable to talk to anyone I kept it inside.

Deciding I needed to finally deal with this once and for all, one Friday when he came to pick me up, I got in the car and had the ring in my hand. It was wintertime and cold outside. Without preamble I stated, "I'm breaking up with you" or something to that effect. "We are kids and too young to get married". Eddie became very angry. Yelling and cursing at me to get out of the car, I did so. He spun out of the approach to the place where we lived. It wasn't a driveway, only a place to pull in at the bottom of the hill where the house was.

Going back into the house I cannot recall anyone specifically saying anything to me, but I'm sure something was said and quite certain I told them what I'd done. There were no meaningful comments made though to my recollection. Relief is the emotion I remember feeling. Like a load had been lifted from my shoulders. Finally, it was over. Little did I know it had only begun. For one evening I was myself again.

After breaking up with Eddie, the next day all went well. Sleeping well for the first time in a long time, it was surprising when his mom and dad pulled in at the bottom of the hill. They came into the house and told my parents they wanted to talk to them in private. Telling me to go to the other room, I had taken sheets and tacked them to the ceiling to map off a corner for the half bed I slept on, and this is where I went. Sitting in there while my fate was being decided, I don't know what was said. All I know is I was pulled out of school, and taken to have my blood drawn for a blood test. To get married a couple had to have a blood test drawn to check for syphilis and any other communicable diseases. I think it took three days. Application for a marriage license was next on the agenda. Those people didn't know how to do much, but they knew how to get married and tell others what to do. That's a judgmental statement but the memory still leaves me dumbfounded.

My wedding day came. My parents didn't attend, only Eddie's parents and a preacher at some little church in a neighboring county. Strange recollection to say the least. Never understanding how it happened I just accepted it and went on trying to be a wife. We moved in with his parents along with everyone else living there, it amounted to nine people living in the household. Eddies parents went to work every day, and we just stayed there at the house. His sister was fourteen years old and pregnant. Her husband had broken his leg playing basketball, so he was in a wheelchair. He probably was drawing unemployment I'm not sure, but it takes a lot of food to feed that many people. Staying clean was difficult. Being used to bathing regularly even though it was in a wash pan, it seemed to me they didn't take cleanliness as seriously as I did. There was no indoor bathroom, so it was such an embarrassing time for me.

Eddie's sister acted like she was grown. She would cook supper each night. Not knowing how to cook or take care of anyone other than myself, she became very hateful to me. She didn't like me, and I didn't like her. She tried to relate to me, but our thinking was so different, there was no way to relate to one another. She had dropped out of school in eighth grade, ready to begin life as an adult and had. On the other hand, here, I am in shock at the way everything has happened to me and unsure how to continue in the spot I found myself.

Shortly after mine and Eddie's marriage she and I went to the laundry mat in Moro, Arkansas. As we were putting our clothes in the dryer, a couple of older women were in there doing their laundry. They struck up a conversation with us. I never had much to say because I was terribly shy. My sister-in-law was a big talker though as was my husband. She engaged them in conversation. They were adults, we were not, and I could tell by the words they were using they were making fun of us. She seemed unable to grasp their tone, continuing with the idle patter she was so efficient at doing. Being two years younger than I perhaps she missed the inferences they were making because she forged ahead. Stating I was newly married to her brother, they replied, "well, they should be on their honeymoon, shouldn't they?" she said, "oh they decided not to go on a honeymoon". I was mortified by the whole incident. When we left, she was fuming. Not knowing what to say or feel about anything, I was mute. It seemed this whole period of my life was being planned by others and I had no opinion, I was just there, playing a role minus a script. Leaving my parents' home to become a child of someone else. Going along with whatever was happening at the time was the only way to survive.

Unable to perform sexually, our wedding night was a disaster. It seemed my pelvic muscles clamped down and would not allow penetration. There had been no instruction in my life about anything as far as education goes about such things, so I didn't know what was wrong. Eddie got mad and threw a fit, cussing me out. I cried and we went to sleep. His sister and her husband had a trailer sitting across the creek from the house where we all lived, and this is where we spent our wedding night. The water wasn't hooked up but there was electricity. I'm not sure why she and her husband didn't stay there.

Deductive reasoning now tells me the conversation Eddie's parents had with my parents was that I was pregnant. We had copulated before our marriage, but I was not pregnant. Figuring it was time to find out what all the buzz was about sex I, in my child's mind thought I'd try it and see. It was not a pleasant experience there on the front seat of the' 64 Chevrolet Impala. He told me he was experienced in this, and I suppose I believed him. Since he was my boyfriend that's what we done. After that it seemed that's all he wanted to do and we stopped doing anything other than him picking me up, taking me to visit his parents and then parking on a side road somewhere and having sex. Declining on my part would cause him to throw a fit. I knew I was in trouble with no place to turn. Well, I say I knew I was in trouble but not in so many words. All I knew was I needed to get out of this mess. This knowledge is what propelled me to break up with him.

I believe he had told his mother I was pregnant because he couldn't face the fact that I'd broken up with him after telling his family we were getting married. His family, as I said was matriarchal so whatever his mother said" carried the day". All his dad would do is throw a fit and maybe go get drunk. As many people are she wanted to give her children what they wanted, and he wanted me so if it took a lie to get whatever it was, she was willing to do it. She believed her children always. No matter what the story was, they all used it to their advantage. Since I was not their child, I was a pawn in the game of someone else's existence. Unable to conceive how far people will go to gain a perceived, temporary want, garnering all resources available to achieve it, I was incapable of dealing with the reality that an innocent trip to the County fair would bring about.

This began a journey of life without a roadmap, just a measurement of things I wanted against things I didn't have along with a way of life I wanted against a way of life I didn't know how to attain. Calling myself unhappy is far from true. Living with people, in their home is not the way I wanted to live though. Wanting my own space, along with wanting more money than we had, which was none, it wasn't that I didn't love these people because I did, it was simply not the life I had envisioned for myself being involved in.

My memory of my oldest sister moving in with my family in my earlier years had caused me to decide that I never wanted to live with anyone or have anyone live with me. Early childhood experiences, evoking a pleasant or unpleasant feeling, guide all of us in the creation of our own existence, not as to a hard and fast right or wrong, rather in the way something feels to us mentally. Having been taught love and acceptance in my upbringing was all I had to work with internally and it was difficult for me to understand the way of life I was confronted with. We were children playing a grown-up game and I didn't know the rules. It seemed there were no rules in their home. The children were allowed to curse and use language I'd never heard people use. They used this language to one another and even to the parents with no chastisement. Notice to education, vocation, and anything that would have made sense to my thinking seemed nonexistent. The lack of encouragement from my own parents in these areas is what got me into this mess. How to put a roof over our heads and feed ourselves was something Eddie and I were incapable of because we were children. His parents seemed more than willing to take on this role of provision for us.

I never doubted I was special and worthy of being loved as the special person I knew myself to be, my life at this time was not a reflection of it. Eddie relegated me to an inferior status. Not being his fault for doing it nor mine for accepting; it was simply a product of the hierarchy of our social system. Just going along with whatever was presented, because I was powerless to make a change in my existence. Wanting more for us, all I encountered was more of the same I had been raised on, want, need, and deprivation. The biggest difference being I was depending on him, and he was depending on his parents. He was a diabetic, had been since the age of six. Having been told he was sick, which was what his mother always said when he had any sort of misbehavior, he had been taught to feel sorry for himself and always catered to. There was animosity toward him from the other siblings and since we had gotten married the animosity was directed at me as well. His sister displayed an open dislike for me. Not knowing how to respond, I just disliked her right back. There seemed to be less love in my husband's household than I had ever been exposed to. We had always said "goodnight, I love you" when we went to bed at my parents' home and these people never said they loved each other or practiced kindness it seemed to me.

Drinking was allowed in the household even though it was a dry county. There were "bootleggers" in the county who made their living selling booze illegally. This is where Eddie went when he left my house. He got drunk, went home and told his parents whatever story he had concocted to get his way, which was he wanted me and him to get married. Now, speculation is all I have as the story told, but the most feasible is the aforementioned story. Throwing a fit was the usual manner of being heard in the household I was married into with the voice of reason being Eddie's mother and her motive was giving her children whatever they wanted. Unknown to me, this was my first lesson in the unfairness of life and without an education or means of support one must accept whatever situation they are in sans any manner or ability to change. Such is the way it is when anyone is at the mercy of lies and deceit.

Even though Eddie's mother got angry when his dad drank, there were times when he would bring beer home and she would drink as well. I was allowed to drink as well as anyone else who happened to be there at the time. She would get in a crying jag, and I would attempt to console her. She was unhappy with her life and the mess she was in having married at fourteen years of age and having five children one after the other until she had miscarried the last one and she was still grieving that. Her woes were endless and unsolvable; hence misery was her companion. Seeking in me a role of friendship, I was incapable of filling because she was a woman, and I was a child. Both she and her husband were decent hardworking people who viewed life in a black and white, right or wrong manner. Not understanding what I was living or observing, it seemed why have all the worry she had, and opt to not take steps to resolve it. Worry and doubt along with blaming others was her constant companion and she accepted it.

Eddie's father heard of a job working on a farm in the community. It was a pig farm. Eddie and I went to talk to the people to interview for it. The pay was one dollar an hour. Furnishing us a place to live and paying for our utilities which was electricity because we used well water, it was a trailer. It was old but nice enough. Having indoor plumbing was a God send after living my whole life without it. Rolling Acres was the name of the farm. Edward Stinnett and his wife were the owners of the farm. Their son Dan and Zona lived on the farm as well. They had adopted four children that I would baby-sit for when she would work, which was sporadically. She was a nurse and would work at Monroe County Hospital occasionally. It was a good arrangement for us all. Eddie worked long hours during the summer because an operation of that magnitude required it. Since he was diabetic and never learned the importance of self-care, he got sick. There was no air conditioning in the trailer, and it was unbearably hot. He would come home for lunch every day, so my job was cooking breakfast and lunch for him. The rest of the time

I would read and make sure the trailer was clean. One day he came home for lunch, and I was reading a book I had gotten somewhere. Rather than eat with him I went to the bedroom, sat on the bed and read. Before he left to go back to work, he came back there and grabbed the book from my hands. Throwing it against the wall he slapped me hard in the face and said never to leave the table again while he was eating. I was supposed to eat with him. When he came home the fight continued. I didn't want to displease my husband, but I did like reading. He said, "I'll take you back to your parents' house where I found you". Crying, on my knees I promised never to do such a thing again.

Dissatisfaction set in, unable to go to work of course we lost our place to live and consequently moved back in with his parents. This would have been in the fall of 1969 or '70. Having enrolled in Monroe County High School, moving back with his parents proved to be too much for me so I dropped out of school once more. My heart had not really been in it anyway. I felt silly being married and going to school. Many girls were doing it during that time and maybe it worked for them, but it didn't work for me. Feeling totally powerless over my life, my spirit was gone. Uninspired and unable to identify with any women I was exposed to I felt no hope of any kind in creating or envisioning a positive mindset of creation. Exposure at that time in my existence was not portraying a pleasing experience of the female gender in general. Probably Zona was closer because at least she was a professional who had gainful employment. Education seemed to be frowned on in my culture, with the only reason people sent their kids to school was because the law said they must. Nearly all children in my family quit school at sixteen or earlier. Girls, to get married or help with the family, boys, to go to work, except in Eddie's family, the kids just quit going, staying home with nothing being said about it by anyone.

Eddie and I went back to living the way we had started out, with his parents and being one of the rest of the kids.

We received a phone call one day from my sister Cheryl. She had heard about our situation, and she said the place where her man Frank worked needed some help. If we could come there, he would get Eddie a job. Deciding to do this, we didn't have a car, so Eddie's dad helped us get one. This car was ancient. It was a 1940 Ford I believe. Maybe not a Ford and maybe older than that, whatever it was we started out in it. Driving up the highway it began to rain. The windshield wipers were vacuum powered and not very good at all. Driving in the stop and go traffic they wouldn't work well enough in the downpour to clear the windshield. Eddie would open his window, lean out, and use his cap to clear it enough to see to drive. Finally arriving at my sisters' house, in a community right outside of Little Rock, on a Friday afternoon, Eddie was scheduled to start work the following Monday, which he did.

The pay was two dollars an hour, so it was double what he had been making but we had to pay rent, utilities, buy groceries and everything else associated with living. Staying with them a couple weeks, maybe a month we saved our money and began perusing the newspaper for apartment rentals in Little Rock. Exciting but scary, we were attempting to make a life for ourselves. Even though I still felt like a child I was full of love and expectation thoroughly excited to be getting a place of my own once again.

Cheryl and Frank had four children and they lived in a small house. It is one of the houses built in 1968 and since he was an army veteran, he was eligible for the G.I. bill to obtain property ownership. Really the house was not big enough for them, but they welcomed us with open arms. Frank was from Hungary, having immigrated during the uprising in 1956, when Hungary was invaded by Russia. The United States accepted 30,000 refugees. He would never talk about it with me even though I asked him to tell me his story. Maybe the experience was too painful to relate. He was a heavy equipment mechanic at a place in Little Rock, owned by two brothers. Eddie began working there as an entry level employee. His duties consisted of cleaning the shop and delivering heavy equipment to job sites or whoever had purchased something from them around the general area.

We found an apartment in what is known as Old Little Rock. Located at 1361 Floyd Street, apartment #4. The rent was 80$ a month and we had to pay for personal electricity. Water was furnished as was garbage pickup. This is still the usual way of things with most apartment rentals. Calling to inquire about the apartment a date was set to go see it. The area was attractive with the building shaped like a horseshoe, having a courtyard in the center with flowers growing in it. We had to pay one month's rent and a deposit of the same amount, along with the deposit for electricity.

It was furnished with a vinyl sage green sofa and chair in the living room, two end tables with lamps, coffee table along with a braided area rug on the floor. Entering there was a musty odor about it but that was because it had been sitting empty. There were hardwood floors throughout except the kitchen had linoleum and the bathroom had ceramic tile. With large windows in the living room and bedroom having tension roll up blinds but no curtains. The wallpaper on the walls and even the ceiling, was in a good state of repair. Directly to the left of the living room was the kitchen furnished with a Formica table and four chairs, apartment sized gas stove, with the water heater adjacent to it. All the pipes hooking the stove and water heater up to gas were visible on the walls. The refrigerator was ancient as there was a ball on top of it with the motor inside, barely enough room to store groceries for the week. The sink was a single sink with two spigots. One for hot water, one for cold. In the bathroom there was a clawfoot bathtub with separate spigots for the hot and cold water as well. The sink drain was visible as there was no vanity, it was just attached to the wall. It was a nice apartment but not modern, circa 1940's.

Moving in on a Saturday, we set about thoroughly cleaning the place. Apartments always seemed dirty to me, knowing others had lived there and most times they were not in the best condition. Eddie was always helpful with housework. By Monday morning we had things done well enough and he went back to work so began our life again in our own place.

Lack always seemed to plague me. We had enough money to pay rent, utilities, and buy groceries but that was all, having no money for decorating the apartment, and I was too young to get a job. Staying there all day without a phone, television or anything to read was not a great existence for me. My job was to clean and cook supper, that was my life at the time. No air conditioning and no money to get one. Nights were hot and we didn't have a fan. We slept with the windows open even though it was downtown. Both of us were secure in our life, never feeling any fear, we soldiered on. Sometimes we would fight as children will do, never anything serious. One fight I recall was on a Saturday. I wanted to go to Dizzy Whiz and get a banana split. Surely, we had the money or else I wouldn't have asked. He said no, becoming angry I began to cry. Eddie became angry and began chasing me. Running down the sidewalk on Floyd Street, with cars going by, he caught me and hit me. Not taking it seriously even then because he had slapped my face when we lived in the trailer, it was acceptable behavior from the male species because that was how I'd been raised. Not expecting others to treat me well, rather taking responsibility for whatever came my way, and not asking for anything. It was my fault for wanting anything.

Lacking any foresight, I never thought of what I felt I deserved, only what he wanted for himself, it was always his call and that is how our life was structured. Feeling an intense responsibility and guilt if anything went wrong there is no wonder, I could not love myself enough to think I deserved good treatment and having whatever I wanted. Was it my youth and immaturity? To this day I cannot answer that question. Depending on Eddie to make all the calls, spend the money as he saw fit with whatever we had left after paying our upkeep, I had gone without decent clothing and shoes so he could save to have the car he had purchased from Frank painted at Earl Scheib paint shop. Training from my youth plagued me by my upbringing. I'm unsure if this is the way to be or not, but we got along okay and had an opportunity to come our way that was beneficial for both of us.

We worked on the body of the Pontiac Le Mans we had bought perfecting any dents or rough spots it had.

Parked on the street because there was no off-street parking everyone saw us doing all this and took notice. One person noticing was the owner of the apartment complex. Sonny and Lucetta Mason were their names. Both were retired from their regular jobs and in their 60's. Seeing our willingness to work to make things better than they were from cleaning the apartment when we moved in because we were outside doing the windows and then doing the body work on the car prompted a visit from Lucetta shortly after we moved in.

I didn't know anyone in the area to visit so I was surprised when a knock came on the door. Opening the door there stood an immaculately dressed woman 62 years old. Her hair was salt and pepper color, styled in the manner of the day when women went to the hairdresser once a week and had their hair done, teased and sprayed into place. Tall of stature, impeccable of dress and manner, is the best description I can manage for her. No nail polish, her nails were filed to a point and buffed to a shine. Her top teeth were capped with gold around the bottom edge. Introducing herself, she asked if she could come in. Of course, I said yes. She told me she was dissatisfied with the resident manager she had, because the man worked the graveyard shift and the woman, his wife, stayed up all night and slept all day. Describing the job requirements, she wanted to know if I was interested in taking it. Telling her I would let her know, I had to talk with Eddie, she gave me her phone number and left.

When Eddie got home from work, I related to him the offer. She had offered our apartment rent free, paying for our utilities, we would have a phone and a window air conditioner. Responsibilities were mowing the grass once a week, collecting the rent, cleaning apartments when people moved, running an ad in the paper when an apartment came empty and showing it to prospective renters. She taught me how to talk to people. Not renting to anyone with children since the apartments were one bedroom it was mostly couples who lived there. The Mortuary College was located nearby, so there were some people going to the school who rented there. Some elderly and a few singles were the remainder of the tenants.

Calling her the following day, I accepted the offer. We lived in apartment four, the resident manager was apartment three, so the move was easy since the apartment was furnished. All I needed to do was move our personal things from one place to the other. I moved us in as soon as the other managers were gone. The place was filthy. Inside the cabinets contact paper on the shelves was black with grime. Cleaning once more before we moved in, it was a better place than where we had come from.

Lucetta called me every day at ten o'clock in the morning. She was like a mother to me. A truly wonderful person. Her vocation had been one of secretary, having worked in the Federal Building, downtown. Her husband, Sonny, had been a merchant marine. She told me he was a self-made man. I didn't know what that meant.

Teaching me how to deal with people, she had a somewhat blunt way about her as far as any tolerance when she was faced with decision making. One such instance, we had rented to a young couple about the same age as Eddie and me. By this time, I was seventeen and Eddie was nineteen. Attempting to be my friend so as to use my phone, every weekday morning this girl would come knocking at my door. Unable to tell her no, she would call someone and stay on the phone for hours. Lucetta, who I called Mrs. Mason would call, and the line would be busy. This was before call waiting so all she would get was a busy signal. Becoming angry, she thought I was on the phone. When I told her what was happening, she said the next time she wants to use the phone, give her a dime and tell her there is a phone booth across the street on the corner. I didn't know how to tell anyone anything, so I done what she told me to, and it worked. When the girl knocked on my door, I gave her a dime and sent her on her way, just as I'd been told to do. What a relief to me because the girl smoked cigarettes and I couldn't stand the smell, so I had to clean the house when she left.

Another incident that occurred was an elderly couple of sisters, living in one of the apartments used paper grocery bags to put the garbage at the back door of their apartment on garbage day. Rather than using garbage bags, which were easier for Eddie and me to carry to the alley for pickup on. Telling Mrs. Mason about it, she told me to tell these ladies they were required to use garbage bags. I told them, yet they continued using paper grocery bags. This is something I regret because I'm sure these ladies were barely getting by financially, yet I continued to hound them about the bags every time they paid their rent. There were twenty-four units in the complex and twice weekly Eddie, and I would collect the garbage from everyone's back door and carry it to the alley, where the garbage truck would pick it up. Using the paper grocery bags, it was not possible to carry more than one bag at a time, rather than several. Lacking discernment as to the possible financial situation of the sisters, if I had it to do over,

I would never have said anything about it to Mrs. Mason, I would have given them some garbage bags.

Things were going well for us. Having more money, we were able to save but we never opened a bank account, I just put the extra money in an envelope and stashed it on the top shelf of the living room closet. Along with Eddies' pay, I got paid extra for cleaning the apartments when people would move out and Mrs. Mason paid me for cleaning the stairways weekly. It was during this time that I began feeling weird physically. Walking down to visit my neighbor, an eighty-year-old lady named Mrs. Wheatly, I told her, "My arms and legs feel disconnected from my body". Laughing she said, "honey, you're pregnant, let me get you a valium." She got me a valium and I took it. Comforting me she told me not to worry, "you're built for having babies," she said. She was happier about it than I was. I was scared and knowing as well that Mrs. Mason would not like it, I went home and took a nap.

Not knowing how to find a doctor, a neighbor of my sister Cheryl recommended one to me. His name was Phillip Kirk. His office was in the west end of Little Rock, not a good area of town. My first visit was terrifying, since I'd never had a pelvic exam before. The receptionist was a chain smoker and Dr. Kirk always had a cigar in his mouth. There was no exam room, rather an exam table in his office behind his desk. With a cigarette dangling from the corner of her mouth, the receptionist held up a dingy sheet as a shield for me to undress and get on the table.

After the exam Dr. Kirk pronounced me pregnant and gave me prenatal vitamins. Leaving the office, the receptionist scheduled me a visit the following month. So began my journey to motherhood.

I became sick. Everything made me sick. Smelling food made me sick as did eating it. Losing weight, I was told in my third month to go to bed and stay there when I began bleeding.

As I suspected, Mrs. Mason was disappointed with my pregnancy. When she visited me the last time, she reminded me of the 'no children' policy she had and told me we had to find another place to live when I got better. She began sending me barley beef soup she made by her husband. Knocking on the door he would say, "here's some soup Lou sent you". I tried eating the soup, but it made me sick as did everything I attempted to eat. Consequently, I wound up with many quarts of soup lined up in my refrigerator. All I could stomach eating was boiled macaroni with butter and black pepper and boiled eggs. Staying in bed was not easy but I was so sick I had to. Finally, I began to recover but Eddie was having a hard time mentally. Recalling a visit from his parents, I was unable to get up and make us something to eat. They went to the store, bought food and his mother cooked lunch. Leaving the food on the table when they left, it sat there until it had molded because I didn't feel like cleaning it up. Eddie was still working, and he didn't clean it so there it sat until I got better. Since they were people of judgement, they were judgmental of me, expecting more of me than I could deliver.

The day I felt like it I ventured to the kitchen and saw the sink overflowing with dishes, a towel covering the food left on the table. Pulling the towel aside, a dish of peas was there with mold covering the top as well as the other items from the meal, but the peas is all I recall. Setting about cleaning up, I spent the day getting things back to normal. My sickness had subsided, and I began assuming my normal duties associated with my job as well as looking for another place for us to live.

Eddie had begun leaving me at the apartment when he visited his parents. Leaving after work on Friday, after coming home, bathing and changing clothes, he would be gone until Sunday evening. Not questioning him, one Friday I remember he started a fight with me because I wanted to go with him. He didn't want me to go. Crying, and begging him to take me, he cussed me out and took the rubber sink stopper and threw it at me hitting me in the chest as he went out the back door. Getting myself together after crying my eyes out, I done the thing that always calmed me, cleaned the house.

The next day, Saturday, Cheryl called and needed me to babysit the four boys while she went to the doctor. Dropping the kids off with me kept me busy chasing them for a few hours, that is how I spent my day. The next day, Sunday, Eddie returned home, and we resumed our life as usual. Nothing was said about the fight or anything else. That's the way it was.

Somehow, I equated the rift between Eddie and me to us having more money. It seemed like when we were barely getting by, we were closer and more loving. Not realizing having more money allowed him to really be himself and fulfill his secret longing to reenact the life he had observed his parents living. His mother had told me his dad had stepped out on her and would leave her home with the kids by herself in the earlier years of their marriage. Of course, Eddie was aware of this behavior because it had become the topic of the many fights they continued to have, and the children picked up on it. Even though Eddie loved his mom he was instilled with the learned behavior of his gender. He was thinking this was the way a man should act. This is the behavior of individuals when they are immature and are victims of the ego. Adulthood is the acceptance of responsibility, not mimicking the adverse belittling of the ones we profess to love.

Later, I found out that while he was taking these weekend trips alone to Monroe County, he had become involved with a little girl living down there. She was only fourteen years old. At the time it was devastating news to me because vows had been broken and our promise to one another had been shattered. Still believing in love and at the time unaware of the discretion, I thought it was having more money, not the character of the person I was married to, causing the rift in our relationship.

There was a fourplex apartment building across the street from where we lived. It was on Woodbine Avenue. Inquiring about a vacant apartment on the second floor of the building, the lady who owned it told me the rent was 40$ a month, along with the usual cost of electricity. It was unfurnished though, and we had no furniture. Non deterred we moved, and the move seemed to revive, in my mind, our relationship. Unknown to me I was witnessing remorse and self-retribution on my husband's part, because I was still in the dark concerning his adulterous act. Forgiveness would have been given and we could have worked through it but something unknown and unacknowledged cannot be forgiven, as life would personally prove to me later, through experience.

The apartment wasn't as nice as the one on Floyd Street. Entering through the door, the living room had large windows directly across from the entrance. It was heated with a gas heater as was the previous apartment, but the layout was different being styled in the manner of a shotgun house. To the right of the entrance was the bedroom, and to the left was a short hallway leading to the kitchen. Midway down the hall was a door on the right to the bathroom. Again, the floors were hardwood in the living room and bedroom, with the bathroom and kitchen having linoleum. There was a small apartment size gas stove in the kitchen but no refrigerator. Applying for a Sears credit card we were accepted and were able to purchase a refrigerator. It was avocado green which was a popular color of the time. It was delivered before we moved in. My sister Joyce who lived in a nearby suburb gave me an orange vinyl sofa. It had a small tear in it but was sufficient. Mrs. Mason gave us a bed and mattress along with a dresser and chest of drawers. In the kitchen someone gave us an unpainted table and two chairs, which I painted white. Working together on the creation of a home caused me to feel like Eddie and I were close again, but I did have continual sadness plaguing me causing me to be tearful and fearful sometimes. Eddie was comforting as well as he could be but the perpetual lack of money prevailed and it seemed we could not provide ourselves with anything other than the basics of livelihood. Wanting to buy things and prepare for the baby I was pregnant with was impossible. Not that I dwelt on this all the time, but I was aware of the lack and it did cause me to be sad. Someone gave us a bassinet, and that was the extent of preparation we made for the birth of my son.

With no phone, I would walk to the phone booth on the corner of Floyd Street. Using a dime, I would call my sisters (Cheryl and Joyce) let it ring once, hang up and they would call me back on the payphone. I had given them the number beforehand. Having moved into this apartment in April of 1972, the absence of air conditioning was not realized yet. Time moved more slowly then it seemed, and the joy of being closer to my husband made life feel good. Saving any change, even pennies, I came up with enough money to walk to the corner grocery and buy bananas one day and made a banana pudding, as a surprise for Eddie. These things made me happy. It seemed as if Eddie always wanted something other than I did. Almost as if simple living and progress wasn't enough for him. He would ask me to do things that were senseless to me. Not accepting the limitations of his age or mine, he wanted us to act older. Sending me to the store on the corner to buy beer was one such thing. He said because I was pregnant, they would think I was old enough to buy it. Being a dutiful wife, here I go to try to buy beer. Of course, they wanted to see my identification, but he had told me to tell them it was for my husband, which I did. They told me to tell my husband to come buy the beer himself.

My days consisted of cleaning the apartment, calling my sisters, watching soap operas and cooking supper for my husband. Since I never learned to cook before marriage, I was not a good cook. Not having a cookbook, I relied on people I knew to tell me how to make food. Passing my time in this manner, I had no friends and little social contact with anyone.

As the months progressed the heat began to become unbearable. Unable to sleep because of the heat Eddie and I would take turns putting rubbing alcohol on a washcloth and wiping one another with it while allowing the box fan to blow on us, this is the way we cooled ourselves to get some sleep.

July 25, 1972, Joyce came to pick me up after Eddie went to work, in her new Ford Pinto. We decided to drive to our mothers' home in Spring Creek for a visit. This is a two-hour drive, each way. Having a nice visit, on our way out to the car, I jumped off the porch which was about three feet off the ground. Mama chastised me for this, saying I should not do this being pregnant. She said it could hurt the baby. After having 15 children my mother knew more than any doctor about childbirth, but I never paid any attention to the things she said. Joyce and I left, making the drive back to Little Rock. Driving up the parkway, we pulled to the side of the freeway to relieve ourselves rather than exiting because we were afraid there would not be an entrance back on. We squatted down behind the opened car door on the opposite side of the traffic. Arriving home before Eddie got home from work, I was exhausted, so I lay down and rested until he got there.

July 26 dawned with a low temperature of 64 degrees. Still tired and feeling sluggish, I went back to bed after making breakfast for Eddie and seeing him off to work. Unable to recognize the onset of labor I knew my back was hurting, but since I'd been away from home the previous day, I felt I needed to clean house. It was a Wednesday.

Realizing now it was the nesting instinct that prompted the urge to clean. After cleaning everything I lay down on the bed to rest. Having to pee, I went to the bathroom. There was a big mucous, ropey like thing emerging from my vagina. It was the plug coming out, but I didn't know that, so I just pulled it out, wiped myself, went back and lay down.

We had only one key to the apartment, and it was to the front door. Eddie used the back door when he came home, since I kept it locked, he had to knock so I could let him in. Having dozed off, knocking jolted me awake. I say awake, but it was more like I was in a daze or stupor. What I was in was labor, but I didn't know it. There had been no instruction at all on what to expect, or what the experience would be like. Mrs. Wheatley was right though, I was built for it because the labor was, painful, but not intolerable. Not until the end.

Opening the door for Eddie, his first words were, "what is wrong with you? "You're white as a ghost ". "I think I need to go to the doctor," I replied. Without entering, he said, "come on, let's go". Making the drive down Broadway to Dr. Kirks office, I was dazed. Upon arrival the receptionist, with the ever-present cigarette hanging from the corner of her lips, ushered me back to his office. Dr. Kirk examined me and said, "you're in labor, get to the hospital immediately, I'll meet you there."

Going back out to the waiting room I relayed what I'd been told, and we began the drive to the hospital, which was about a twenty-minute drive. During the drive I was moaning and rising off the seat holding my son in until we could get there. Upon arrival we were met by an orderly, pushing a wheelchair, and they immediately took me to delivery. Bending forward they injected me with something in my lower back removing all pain. Forty-five minutes after getting to the hospital, at 9:45 p.m. my son made entrance into the world. Looking at him for the first time I was overwhelmed with so many emotions all at once. Not being able to identify anything I was feeling, and no one there except the staff, I cried myself to sleep.

The nuns made their rounds blessing me in the evening. I was not catholic, but it was a catholic hospital Dr. Kirk used. Each night I was there I was in tears when they visited. Sitting on the side of the bed, they prayed for me, and it made me feel better while they were there, but as soon as they left, I began weeping again. I didn't know how to be a mother. I didn't know how to take care of a baby. The nurse would bring him to me to feed and I was terrified for his safety. Breast feeding was being discouraged during this time, so I was given something that was supposed to dry up my milk production, but it didn't work. I wasn't the only young mother there, so the second day I was there the staff took all of us and gave some instruction on how to bathe our child and general care.

Eddie visited me before going to work and when he got off work. This was the only visitor I had. We had not discussed a name for our baby, so I was totally unprepared when they came to my bedside and asked me what I wanted to call him. Feeling pressured to immediately give a name, I couldn't think of anything to call him, so I simply named him after his dad. It all seems crazy now. I don't think I realized the facts of my existence then, nor the impact of parenthood. Just going along with the manner of accepting whatever situation I found myself. Weighing 6 pounds, 15 ounces, my baby was healthy, and I was glad but the fear of being unable to care for him prevailed. My love for him was so overpowering it was disempowering. Eddie and I were so poor I was unsure we could provide for him since we were scarcely able to provide for ourselves. I didn't want to leave the safety of the hospital. After three days I was released and sent home. My son had small casts put on his feet to hold them straight because when he cried, he became too tense and pulled them up to rest on his calves and Dr. Kirk said it would cause them to not grow properly.

Going home to Woodbine Avenue I stayed in bed because the soreness from birth made walking across the floor painful. It was on a Saturday, so Eddie was off work and stayed with me until Monday morning. Calling the baby Gary, he would wake me crying and I could hear the little casts clicking together as he kicked his legs. Eddie took care of us for the next couple days and then it was me and my son there alone. It was an all-day job for me to care for him. His skin was too sensitive to wear pampers, so cloth diapers were used. Since we had no washer and dryer, I washed things in the bathtub. Soaking the soiled diapers in a plastic bucket after rinsing the mess out in the toilet.

When Gary was two weeks old, we decided to take a trip to visit family. Eddie and I went first to see his family, then on down to visit my mine. Somehow it became custom for him to drop me off at my parents then he would go back and spend the night with his family while I spent the night with mine. I never questioned any of his choices or decisions. Returning on Sunday to pick me up we went home. Once there we went to the laundromat which was a once-a-week chore as was grocery shopping. While folding the clothes I had Gary in a carrier sitting on the folding table. Looking at him I noticed he was extremely red in color and touching him he was hot to the touch. I knew something was wrong and it scared me. Collecting our clothes, we hurried home. I used a rectal thermometer to check his temperature and it was 104 degrees. Immediately we took him to the emergency room. They called my doctor. Doing a spinal tap on Gary, he informed me he had viral meningitis. Watching through a plate glass window as my baby lay on an exam table and a needle was inserted into his lower spine to remove fluid for testing. It was a horrific experience. Bringing him to me after the procedure I was able to feed him, and he ate hungrily from the bottle.

Feeling as if my incompetence caused my son to get sick, Dr. Kirk assured me that it was not my fault but that did not assuage the guilt

I felt when he was admitted to the hospital for a two-week period. Since I had been at my parent's house from Friday till Sunday, with no indoor plumbing, no screens on the doors and general unsanitary conditions, are more likely the reason he got sick. Nothing was explained to me as the cause of such a thing happening, it was only many years later I was able to research and find out the main cause of this condition is lack of sanitation. The strong antibiotics given to him to counteract the virus I was told could cause his baby teeth to be discolored and his head might grow larger than his body. His baby teeth were slightly discolored but that was the only after effect he had. Taking him home was a joyous occasion for me. I reveled in my love for him.

Eddie always wanted to include his family in our life even though our resources were limited. His younger brother visited us often spending a couple weeks at our apartment. Edde got paid biweekly, so it was on pay week we would go to see our families. His brother always peed the bed even though he was a teenager. It was a medical problem I'm sure but without a way to wash bedclothes I began to detest the visits because there was no way to keep the smell down plus it was embarrassing for me and him. It was never discussed at all, just pretend it wasn't happening. At the time I was doing this with all the events in my life. Living someone else's dream but certainly not my own, I accepted everything and asked for nothing in return. Attempting to honor my marriage vows by adhering to my upbringing, I never thought my actions or behavior had any bearing on my existence. As is said hindsight is 20/20, so I just went along with my husband. Not realizing how my behavior was thought of as being stupid.

Eddie had wanted to drink alcohol. By this time, he was old enough to buy beer and did when he had the money. He began including me more in his life and being young and inexperienced I went along. One such time proved a point a long time in coming. We had been to visit his family and his brother had come home with us. Being on a Sunday, we watched television and drank beer. His brother and I were sitting on the couch. Since Eddie had to work the next day, he went to bed. My feet were on his brother's lap. We were just hanging out and talking when he began rubbing himself with my foot. Surprised, I immediately went to bed, but a seed had been planted in my mind. As silly as it seems now, at the time I was shocked at this. Unbelievable to me, I went to bed and went to sleep.

Next morning after Eddie left for work, before Gary woke up, I went to the living room and lay with him on the couch. I had never had anyone want me physically other than my husband and it was somewhat exciting to think about. Not even an adult yet and very immature we went on and had sex. I think it only happened once that day, but I had broken my vows and promises I'd made so it wasn't long before self-denigration began with me. As with the bedwetting, what we had done was not talked about. The straying on my part sprang from not having any life goals and a feeling of ennui felt after the birth of a child that I felt unprepared for.

My husband I felt had absolute trust in me, but hindsight tells me different. Perhaps there was another energy at play, there is no way for me to know. What I do know is his brother fell in love with me and again this was never talked about. He would show up unannounced at the apartment, without Eddie going after him. He was the one who told me about the girl Eddie was seeing while I was pregnant. This was his justification for his behavior.

Gary was thriving and healthy and he was the only true love I had in my life. Thinking my life would always have the love of my child in it, lacking any foresight I could not imagine the wild ride I was about to take.

Wandering from the path of my promises made in my wedding vows, my mind wandered as well. Rather than focusing on the wellness of my baby, I simply took it for granted. My mind knew what was happening was wrong but even as I knew my getting married when I didn't want to was wrong, I just went along with whatever was happening. Guilt began to chase me, and I couldn't run fast enough to get away from it. When we went to Monroe County, I stopped going to my parent's house to stay all night and started staying at Eddies parents. Going with him to ballgames and whatever he came up with to do. We were acting our age, yet not acting as responsible parents. We both were still children. Children trying to raise children, it was the blind leading the blind.

What had filtered down to me as a child from the way I was raised was an either-or way of being. Life was black or white, good or bad, right or wrong. Never any in betweenness or acceptance of anything other than perfection. Rigidity, causing me to pass harsh judgement on myself as unforgiveable along with a feeling sorry for my husband and child for having someone such as myself in their life. Needing someone to share my thoughts with, yet cursed with the undeniable urge to procreate, I can only be thankful I did not become pregnant. With the way things unfolded from this point on I was drawing only negativity to myself, and it came full force.

Not knowing how to move past the situation I was in, I just continued to continue. Inability to use my words to articulate how I was feeling, and no person in my life to share with, I kept all this inside, eating away at me.

Hating myself for the betrayal of my marriage vows, I began to feel unworthy of being a parent or wife. Drowning in self-hate I didn't know which way to turn. All I could do was keep up the charade of being a dutiful wife but inside I was sick. My patriarchal upbringing dictated I please my husband but what about this behavior that was happening that seemed beyond reproach. Unable to run his brother off from the home we had created, I'm unsure where fault lies. Hormones are powerful energies. Curiosity from inexperience as well as having life thrust on me in ways that I was unprepared for is the best I can come up with.

Going to visit Eddies family one weekend in 1973, it was springtime. Deciding to go to a ballgame at the high school, we went to my parents and picked up my brother, two years younger than me, as a date for Eddie's younger sister. His brother went as well. Along the way we got some beer from a bootlegger. Once at the game his brother met a girl he knew, and we decided to give her a ride home. All of us were drinking alcohol. This was the life we were living at the time. We had left Gary with Eddie's mother, thank goodness. Leaving the game, Eddie asked his brother to drive. The car was the Pontiac we had bought from Frank, Cheryl's husband. My brother, Eddie's sister, Eddie and I were in the backseat. His brother and his date were in the front. Speeding down the road toward Eddies parents' home, we passed the turn to take us to his parents and continued down the highway to the next town. There was a road that would take us back to our destination from there. We made it to the turn off. These roads were narrow and crooked, not roads to be speeding on. Hearing the weeds hitting the side of the car, I knew we had left the road. Overcorrecting, to pull back on the road we hit a tree dead center of the vehicle. Dazed I climbed out and made it to the roadway. Eddie's sister was already there. My pant legs were wet, and I couldn't figure out why until I touched my head and looked at my hands and they were covered with blood. I was in shock. Seeing car lights, we both began waving our arms to stop the oncoming car. It was my uncle who lived down the road from where the accident had happened. He put us both in his backseat and took us to the county hospital. The hospital dispatched an ambulance to the scene of the accident to retrieve the others. This accident added to my feelings of guilt and worthlessness because of the love for my brother being with us and his getting hurt. His injuries were the worse ones of any of us. I was kept overnight, everyone else was treated and released, but my brother had a two-week hospital stay. It seemed everything around me was falling apart and I'm only nineteen years old. Unreal as all this was there was no progress being made, and we kept winding up where we had started, living with his parents. All this proves the thoughts we engage in draw to us the things that happen. Not realizing any of my power to create I was like a ship atoss in a raging storm on the ocean. Fear was an ever-constant companion, and I blanked out any thought other than survival. Eddie lost his job; the car was totaled, and it seemed he was proud of these things. Mortified at the way my life was going, I still could not find any words to express how I felt, just trudged along. His brother left me alone for a while after this and it felt like maybe that part was over with until Eddie got sick with his diabetes and had to be hospitalized, leaving me there on my own and sleeping upstairs in one of the two bedrooms that was up there. His brother was in one room, Eddie and I in the other room. Going to bed after getting home from the hospital I went upstairs. His brother wasn't there so I went to sleep. Shortly after dozing off, I heard someone climbing the stairs. Rather than going to his bedroom, he came to where I was sleeping. He was drunk. Conceding because I didn't know how to do otherwise, after he finished, he got up and went to his bedroom. My onslaught of disgust for myself continued, even though I didn't know what I was feeling. My life was far removed from any imagination I might ever have had.

Eddie got out of the hospital, and we began looking for a place to rent. Spring Lick is a rural community in Monroe County. We found an old house there to rent. The rent was ridiculously cheap, maybe 10$ a month or something like that. We moved all our things from the apartment on Woodbine Avenue to this house. We only stayed there at night. As soon as we got up, we would go to his mother's house, spend the day and return to this house to sleep. I didn't even try. My sister, four years older than me, and her family had rented a house a couple of doors down from this place and she made a home of it but somehow, I couldn't muster the energy to attempt. No indoor plumbing, no heat other than a stove in the front room, it reminded me too much of the poverty I was trying so desperately to escape. Simply existing in the winter of 1973, misery was a constant companion.

Spring came and with-it renewed life. Eddie and I found a small house right up the road from his mom's and the rent was 15$ a month. He must've been getting unemployment, but I don't know where we got the money, but we rented this place. It had a front room and back room, a good well of water and I made the place look nice. The floors in the front room were hardwood and the room was large enough to separate into a bedroom and living room. The orange vinyl sofa acted as a room divider, and I put linoleum on the front half and painted the rear half a light brown color for the bedroom. In the kitchen we had the green refrigerator and an apartment size gas stove that we got bottled gas to operate. Along with our table and chairs we were outfitted with all we needed. A baby bed sat in the front room to the right of the entrance door, but Gary never slept in it, he always slept with us. I found a sturdy stick straight enough to use as a rod and from one corner of the living room to the opposite wall nailed it to the wall to serve as a closet to hang our clothes on. Creating a place for us, we still went to his mother's house, but it was pleasant enough at home once the weather warmed up. I began staying at home more. Gary and I played, and I enjoyed him more during this time than I can ever recall.

Eddie's mom worked as a domestic for some families in town. Her back went out and she couldn't go to work. She suggested to her employers as a replacement and to ensure she had a job when she got better that I take over until her back healed, so I did. Eddie's dad would pick me up on his way to work in the mornings and drop me off at whichever place I was to clean that day. Pay was 1$ an hour so it amounted to 8$ a day, or 40$ a week. Having an income assisted us in having a little extra over what we had before. Being busy helped me in more ways than one. It kept me away from the house and kept me from being alone, which disallowed his brother having any access to me. The guilt was still there but the more distance created the better.

It wasn't long before Eddie's mother was better and was able to return to work. I was happy not to have to get up so early and leave the house but did miss the money. Soon after this happened, we got a call from Frank, Cheryl's man. She had left him, and he needed help with the four boys since he had to work and had no reliable childcare. His offer was he would get Eddie's job back for him if we returned to Little Rock and I would watch the little ones while he went to work. We accepted the offer. He needed someone immediately, so we packed up and returned to begin again where we started from initially.

Frank found out that Cheryl was at my parent's home in Lee County shortly after we arrived. When the weekend came, he and Eddie made the trip down there Friday evening after work to retrieve her. Staying there with the children I was sitting at the table when they returned. Immediately they went to the back of the house, and I never even spoke to her. We continued in this manner for a period, until as before Eddie had gotten a few paychecks and we had saved enough money for an apartment.

Calling Mrs. Mason to see if she had anything available since she owned another apartment building other than the one, we had been managing. She said her sister-in-law owned an older apartment and had a vacancy. Giving me the number of this woman, I called and set up a date to look at the apartment. It was on Third Street in Little Rock. It was an older home that had been turned into apartments.

The woman lived on the third floor and worked as a bookkeeper for a law firm downtown. She was elderly and wore her gray hair in a low bun on the back of her head. Dressing in all black, her shoes were the type of shoe elderly women wore at that time, having a two-inch square heel and laces, black in color. Gruff and matter of fact in demeanor is my recollection of her. Totally different than Lucetta, she seemed to not care about her looks.

Renting the first floor it consisted of a large living/dining area that had a non-functioning fireplace in it as did the bedroom. Pocket doors separated the living/ dining area, and the place was furnished with antiques. There was a somewhat galley kitchen with the bathroom off from it. Once more we had a place to call home. Setting about cleaning the place it took a month before I was comfortable cooking and eating there.

Settling back to a routine as before except I had Gary to care for and we enjoyed one another immensely. Taking a walk each day around the neighborhood he would run ahead of me looking back to see if I would give chase, which I always did. Our money was the same but with my child it seemed I was more content.

One day there was a knock at the back door. Answering, it was Eddie's brother. My feelings were neither hatred nor blame. Internalization of all the responsibility for what I had done, I allowed him to enter. We sat on the floor of the bedroom and played with Gary. When I put Gary down for a nap the same behavior began again, and I felt there was no escape. My confusion was at the point that, should I refuse and make him leave the "cat would be out of the bag" and if I go along, I'm going to hell. Rectification, justification or faultfinding with anyone other than myself never entered my mind. Doom and damnation are the emotions I felt. Disgust at the incident and myself. The stage was being set for the way I continued to deal with things for many years following. Taking responsibility for any mishap and blaming myself, I invited all manner of abuse by self and others.

Deciding I needed to get a job so I could get out of the mess I was in and accepting the fact that I was an unfit person, not deserving of love or anything other than the misery I had created, I began looking for a job in the help wanted ads of the Courier Journal newspaper. With only a tenth-grade education and never considering I could learn whatever I needed to know to perform a job of my choosing I only considered the most menial vocation available. Because of childcare I had to work nights so Eddie could care for our son. My considerations were limited, not thinking about my need for sleep, I was only looking for a way to stop the guilt and misery I carried within. Finding an ad for waitress at the Western Pancake House on Broadway, not far from where I lived, the shift was from eleven o'clock at night till seven o'clock in the morning. My skills were limited since this was the first attempt at serving and the training offered was nonexistent. Just go out on the floor and wait on people. Our clientele were the people who roam the streets at night, after certain hours. Pimps and their girls would come in around three o'clock in the morning, dressed to the nines. This was the seventies, so the men wore big colorful hats with plumes or feathers on them. The women wore high heels and were dressed fashionably. There was a spot in downtown where these people walked the streets calling to people in cars, asking men if they wanted a date.

My pay was the going rate at the time for a waitress, of one dollar an hour. Since I was inexperienced at my job and relating to the people I served, my tips were not good. The best shift to work was the morning shift. Unable to sleep during the day because I had a toddler, I was tired. Eddie decided to bring his younger sister to our apartment to look after Gary while I slept. She was fourteen years old. It was not a good fit for me. Awaking at two o'clock in the afternoon, my front door was open, and my son was in the foyer of the building by himself, while she was on the porch talking to a male person I had never seen before. She meant no harm, but I was not happy with the situation. Telling Eddie when he got home from work that she could stay the week, but I didn't want her to watch my boy, so we took her home and I went back to napping when Gary took a nap and when Eddie got home from work.

Gnawing guilt still plagued me. Turning twenty was a milestone age for me. Looking in the mirror one day I decided, my only escape from guilt was a divorce because of my unworthiness. Having nobody to talk with about my decision, I looked in the phonebook to find an attorney to file the necessary paperwork. Eddie knew nothing about my decision. We never talked about things like that. I also felt I needed to move, so I went through all my clothing, discarding most of it so as not to be reminded of my life there. I was trying to right the wrongs in my life by removing myself from the ones I had deceived. I didn't mean to deceive them, nor do them wrong, it was the nature of my curiosity about life and immaturity, along with lack of guidance by anyone other than my young husband who was in over his head himself. He was a good person, but we were ill matched. Holding myself to standards set by my parents and not knowing about worldly things, I imagined I needed to be punished for my gross infraction. Freedom was what I was seeking, and love and acceptance based on truth, not a pretense that all was well when it was not. Again, the inability to use words to convey myself and ease the dis-ease inside.

Ms. Mason, the owner of the building where we lived had a small vacant apartment at the back of the entrance hall. The door to the place was unlocked so I went in to check it out. There had been no one living in it since we had moved in. Rent on it was 40$ a month. Thinking I could make it paying that much, I asked her if I could rent it. We agreed, so I moved in. It was furnished. Not as nice as where we were living but it would suffice. Entering through the door it was a straight shot through. No living room but the kitchen then a bedroom with a full-size bed taking up most of the room, having just enough room to walk around it. A step up from the bedroom contained a claw foot bathtub, sink and commode. Eddie and I had begun taking Gary to a daycare down the street from us so I could sleep during the day. Blame of myself along with guilt was tangible in my psychic. Feeling these negative emotions, I was unsure how anyone could not see the pain I was in. Telling my husband of the pain I was in was impossible. Having nowhere to turn I took what I thought was the only way out, and that was dissolution of my marriage. Hiding my emotions because I couldn't think the abhorrent thoughts running through my head, the day I moved I invited Eddie to come and eat after he got off work. Attempting to be kind and civil, he was immersed in convincing me not to do what I was doing. Unable to see past my pain and tell him I was an unfit person to love or build a life around, I could not be convinced. It seemed he enjoyed talking about me leaving. All I recall him saying was "I don't want to have Gary tossed from pillar to post, and that is what will happen if you do this". His attempt at wisdom angered me. Had he said, "I love you and don't want you to leave," it would have made me feel better, like I was wanted, but him always trying to act so wisely angered me. Refusing to listen to him I closed myself off even more. Unknown how it would have been received had I come clean to him the real reason for my leaving I've often wondered how it would have gone. Maintaining my stance was all I knew how to do.

Still believing in the possibility of creating a better life, the realness of my existence had not fully been realized to the extent of knowing prophesy made by someone was their take on life and hence by actions made by them would manifest into a reality of their own making. Is it life dictating or is it true? His prophecy was one of destruction for my son and it is beyond me why a parent would do that. He truly believed his words. As for myself, I was immersed in misery of my own making unable to think anything other than the limiting thoughts of my infraction and wanting to make it go away. Stagnant in my thinking, movement needed to be created and action was the only way I could comprehend to cause anything to happen.

No one really wants to create pain for another, it is simply that they are in so much personal pain that it radiates from them in a manner that attracts the same emotion from another person. This is why there is such dissension among the mating of individuals causing a high divorce rate. Focusing on the behaviors leading to divorce is the improper approach. Rather, focusing on the solution would be more of the answer. Stop it before it happens through honest open dialogue. Causing both parties to be on the same page as to the hopes, dreams, and creation of a progressive life for both people involved. Lack of love is not the culprit, but lack of honesty along with a presentation of the way for everyone to thrive. It is impossible to teach progressive thought when a people are consumed with thoughts of survival or the selfishness of having everything be one way, sans discussion of whether happiness will be the product. People change always. Change is the only constant and not acknowledging this fact will ensure disaster. Demanding a person to be any way other than they are, is ridiculous, yet this is why dissolutions happen. Courage is not loud nor boisterous, rather a quiet movement in the direction of creating, albeit shakily, along the path of finding a place of palatable existence. Not having an answer for others but a demonstration of how a thing be done. Anything other than this is mimicry of others' behaviors. If happiness and contentment is not what is being experienced with needs met and progress made how can generations move forward?

My thoughts concerning myself were a set decision. I had decided I was worthless and undeserving of anything other than the degradation of sin. This is the best explanation I can conjure to explain the next unfolding chapter of life.

Part Two —————

Fitting into the atmosphere of working of the Pancake House was difficult. Feeling like I didn't fit in or belong there. Again, I chastised myself for being less than. Less than what I didn't know. Unknown to me still was the way men view women. True statement. Wanting truthfulness and honesty to be a mainstay is the thing I wanted to offer, yet self-protection and perceived undeservedness caused a split in my consciousness attracting the same from another.

Always looking young for my age at twenty I must've looked like a twelve-year-old. Attracting the attention of a young man who came in every morning to eat breakfast, how it came about that he asked me anything is long forgotten, yet he did ask me out, He was movie star good looking. Maybe I was as well, that's what people tell me, but my self-assurance and confidence did not match my looks. He was a professional, which was impressive to me, not just a job. Being a few years older than me, I thought he was old. His name was Warren Farnsley. How could anyone of his stature be interested in someone like me? I was swept off my feet by the attention. Thinking so little of myself, I was easy pickings. Confiding in a coworker his asking me out she stated, "if you don't go out with him, I will." This statement prompted me to agree to meet him after work.

Showing up at my work when he got off work himself, we sat in the back of the restaurant and talked. To me it felt good to be free of my guilt and to be manufacturing a dialogue free of constraints. My immature mind did not know the danger that lay ahead for me. All I was aware of was here was someone who lit up when he saw me and seemed enthralled by my presence. It seemed an easy way to erase my past mistakes and start over with a clean slate, bridging the gap of meshing my thoughts of who I professed to be with who I really was. I didn't want to be a cheater and adulterer.

We were both married. His wife worked in the daytime, he worked rotating shifts, so we progressed quickly with our relationship. I was wanting to build a life with him, and he was wanting to have sex with me. He told me he was getting a divorce, and his wife didn't want one so that was our commonality. They had a son six months older than Gary, so another thing in common. It seems inane now but that was the basis for our getting together and deciding to move in together. With no identity of my own and no dreams of a future self, my patriarchal teaching of just doing what the man said reared its ugly head and I listened to him and believed.

Telling him where I lived, he came to my apartment after he got off work and we consummated our relationship. Meanwhile, I had deserted my previous life with the idea I could start over without any qualms. I was going to do everything right this time and not do things to cause me grief. Imagining Eddie would work with me as far as seeing Gary, little did I know the vindictiveness people will exact when they don't get their way. Not wanting to be married in the first place to him, and the way it had happened, was the real reason for the unfolding of things as they did. Carrying this thought along with the only real love I had was for my son, little did I know my son would be used as a tool to hurt me for years to come.

Warren and I met at my work on an off day for us both and went for breakfast, then drove to a state park and made out. The red flags were presenting themselves from the get-go, but my inexperience caused me to ignore them. Going in the restaurant his indecisiveness about where to sit caused me to notice, but not comment when we moved numerous times. Not once or twice but five or six. It was starting to be embarrassing to me. Finally, he settled on a spot. Dutifully I followed along. His indecisiveness had presented itself at my work when he and his partner came in for breakfast, but again I ignored it. He would repeatedly change his order from breakfast food to soup to salad. Once we left the restaurant and drove to the park, all he wanted to do was engage in sexual activity. Talking was out of the question. There was no satisfaction for him. Again, I did not pass any judgement or think there was a problem with him, I accepted his behavior not knowing things would not change, that was the way he was. Carnal was his innate nature, never growing past it. His looks carried the day, and I did make excuses to myself about his way of being. His looks had carried him with any of his achievements up to that point in his existence, so being too hard on myself for my naivety is forgivable but the things endured in this relationship is difficult to digest even now. He had been in the military and had an honorable discharge. His job was impressive while in the military as he was a driver for dignitaries and had a clearance to the White House. Deciding on a career change and then achieving that was impressive to me as well, since I had never known anyone to decide to do anything and make it happen. Listening to him, he said he would help me get a better job and wanted me to leave the Pancake House because all his associates went there. There was a place on the other side of town, a pizza place he thought would be safer than working downtown. Going along with his suggestion I went and talked to the manager and was hired immediately.

We, rather he, rented an apartment. They were new and had central air. I'd never had central air before and it was so nice to be cool in the hot weather. Moving in together quickly, within a month of meeting, changing jobs, and having my son only on my off days was tremendous changes for me and my son as well. Eddie was working with me up to this point as far as visitation went. All these changes caused me to go into shock and my functioning ability declined. Continuing to work as a server, I was on autopilot. Nothing made any sense to me. Warren had self-control issues culminating in jealousy of my two-year-old son and demanding I stay in the bedroom with him while Gary watched television in the living room. Dependent as I was financially, I zoned out and was numb to everything. Shame and guilt plagued me, and I was unable to think cognitively. Too much too fast and my mind couldn't keep up.

Warren and his wife had started building a house before he had filed for divorce, and she had moved there when it was completed. After a month of living together in the apartment she had decided she couldn't afford the house and wanted him to take it, which he did. We moved from the apartment into the house. He paid his child support, but I didn't get child support because Eddie had taken Gary and convinced me to resign my rights as his mother. Since my self-esteem was at an all-time low, I truly felt removal from this earthly existence was my only out. Unable to defend myself against any of the onslaughts coming my way, I still wanted to create a better life, I just didn't know how. Talking to my divorce attorney he said the best thing to do was for me to get married to Warren and petition the court for restoration of my parental rights by showing I could provide a better life for my son than Eddie could. That is how I came to get married for the second time. Waiting until Warrens' divorce was final, we went a justice of the peace and got married.

Going without seeing my son was pure torture for me. Unable to eat, still working at the pizza café, the smell of the place was nauseating. More than once after eating I would go throw up the food and return to the floor to serve customers. The tips were not good, probably because the personal situation I was dealing with prevented me from learning how to interact well enough to cause the customers to like me. Warren wanted to do the right thing he just didn't know what the right thing was. I didn't either for that matter. We were adrift in an ocean of ignorance. My lawyer wanted five hundred dollars to do the court petition to restore my parental rights and Warren paid it. It was all a waiting game and my not knowing how things work, nor the meanness of people, caused me to be unprepared for the onslaught of situations coming my way. Warren had a volatile emotional condition causing him to equate love with jealousy and ill treatment all the while attempting to solve all my problems. Eddie's professed love manifested as hatred and vindictiveness. Before we got a court date on my petition, he sued Warren for alienation of affection because of my leaving him. What a crazy mess. Warren became frightened he would lose his job from an investigation, so he began to find fault with me.

Still working at the pizza place for a dollar an hour, Warren knew a man who was doing some work for a machine shop downtown. The year was 1974 and they had only began hiring women, so he secured an interview for me with a friend of this man, who happened to be the plant superintendent, I was hired. So much happening all at once my mind felt like a ping pong ball bouncing back and forth. These were all major life stressors before I even knew such a thing existed. Didn't even know the word stress nor what it meant. Uneducated, and unschooled in the ways of the world, with only my home teaching to rely on, I mustered on through. Working second shift in the deburr department, using a file to remove the "burrs" left on the parts after being cut with a milling machine, the work was boring, but the pay was good. It was a union shop, so I became a member of the United Steel and Aerospace Workers union, or something like that. Might have been the United Autoworkers and Aerospace workers union, anyway it was a great opportunity for me at the time and I was grateful.

My attorney knew how it would turn out with me going to court on the restoration of my rights, but he had to sell his services. The judge of course ruled in my favor. With my marriage and good job versus Eddie having quit his job and moved back to Monroe County with his mother it was a no brainer but when one is faced with the loss of a child the brain takes a back seat to fear. The call from my attorney telling me the judge ruled in my favor came before going to work, so I had to wait for the weekend to go pick Gary up. This was a happy day for me, more than happy, it was jubilant. A letter had been sent to Eddie informing him of the ruling, so when Saturday came, he was fully aware of my trip to retrieve my son. Warren accompanied me, which perhaps was a mistake, but things can never be known until they happen. Pulling into the driveway, Warren kept the car running while I went on the porch and knocked on the door. Eddies' mother answered and I saw Gary peeking out from behind her. He had snot running out of his nose and was skinny as could be, my love for him rose in my chest and what happened next, I was totally unprepared for. She walked out onto the porch. Pushing me aside, closing the door behind her, refusing to allow me to even touch my son. All the hostilities of her repressed life came spilling out as she pointed her finger at Warren and said, "you need to get back up there where you came from and be a winner up there, we run things down here," or something to that effect. My heart sank, again I had no rights, it was a replay of others calling the shots in my life, inflicting their wishes on me with no concern for how I felt or the pain I was in.

Disappointment is not a strong enough word to describe my mental state. Returning home and work was something done because it had to be. This was the existence I created, wanting more than I'd had, yet it seemed all I wanted now was the thing I'd had. Being with my son took precedence of all my thoughts. My ability to sleep and eat sustained me, but my mental state was remiss. It was all I thought about. Contacting my attorney, he calmed me assuring me there was something to be done and we would do it. All this took more time though and it was again hurry up and wait. Taking a toll on me and my son as well. These people showed me how mean they could be when they had the upper hand. Evil is the word coming to mind. Their actions were inconsequential, and a mere reflection of the depravity others will deflect, to get their way even though they don't know what their way is. Meanness to someone because that person decides they want something for themselves other than what they have planned for them.

Once again it was petitioning the court to file a motion of contempt, get a court date set and more waiting. All the while my son was not receiving the care he needed and was living in less than stellar conditions. Listening to a false narrative describing me to gentle ears and forming brain of a child.

Finally, the court date arrived. It was a harrowing experience for me and in hindsight the lawyer Eddie and his mother hired had probably done it for a good laugh. How can anyone be sued for alienation of affections? All this fiasco was absolutely embarrassing for me. Not only that but it caused Warren to question whether we had done the right thing by getting married. He was thinking out loud, but it still created a misunderstanding on my part about the whole mess. He was put on the witness stand and questioned as to his intent for me. The judge ruled in our favor of course, but I still didn't have my son. A date was set for me to go back to Monroe County to pick Gary up. When Warren and I went to get him, he of course wanted to sit in my lap. These were the days before car seats for toddlers, so he had to sit in the backseat because Warren was jealous of him. He lay down in the seat and wanted to hold my hand. Holding his hand caused Warren to become angrier and demanded I stop. Attempting to keep the peace I removed my hand from my baby son's hand. Having already seen the fits Warren could throw, I didn't want to experience it again.

Arriving home I had to go to work that evening, so Gary had to go to the sitter who lived a few houses down from me. Picking him up when I got off work, I bought him a candy bar. We played, I tickled him, and we had so much fun. Thinking I could now be a mother and display love to my child, it was a rude awakening when Warren became insanely jealous of him. Refusing to allow me to go to him when he would cry out during the night, Warren would go himself and instill terror in his little heart and mine as well. Not knowing what to make out of it, again I was dealing with things I was unprepared to deal with. I couldn't comprehend how anyone could mistreat a two-year-old child. Not knowing the way mental illness presented itself, I took offense to it and decided to talk to Warren about his actions. Spanking and leaving bruises as well as making him eat was behavior I had never experienced anyone having before and I knew it was wrong. Talking with him about his actions did not go well. His anger and inability to manage himself caused things to get worse. Of course, when his son visited, he made a difference in the treatment of them, and I would not allow that to happen. If one child had to clean their plate, both must. Not saying it was the way to handle things, but he had crossed lines with me, and I was ready to fight, the only thing was I couldn't fight him physically only mentally. Any sort of behavior he exhibited to Gary I demanded he do the same to his son. I didn't do this with words, rather looks and somehow as dense as he was, he got the message. Finding things out firsthand has always been a weakness of mine. Hearing someone say something is a certain way, was never enough for me, I wanted to see for myself. Stepchildren portrayed in nursery rhymes was the only exposure I'd had; little did I know I was experiencing it firsthand. Abuse happens across the board, even in families with the same birth parents but I didn't know anything about separation of minds and life experience causing people to act in adverse ways. It seemed to me we had everything anyone would want, so why can't we just be happy? Not so, it could not be.

Continuing with my life was all I knew how to do. Warren was a sex addict among other things. Things he thought about he shared with me to my dismay. Exposure to his thoughts was scary for me but his cognition of how anyone else felt about anything took a backseat to him. He fantasized about group sex, taking drugs, and anytime he made an arrest for prostitution he would bring the mug shot of the girl home to show me. One girl he was enamored with. He wanted to take pictures of me in suggestive ways dressed as he would dress me. Assenting to his wishes, since kodak had made a camera where the pictures developed themselves, so they didn't need to be sent anywhere for development. As far as participating in deviant sexual behavior I was able to convince him it might not be a thing we'd want to do because of his job. My existence at this time was fraught with unease because his behavior was something I had never encountered and didn't know how to deal with. Placating him was impossible, it seemed he was haunted by misery and abusing others was the only way he had to escape its grip, and the escape was only momentary. Having no one to ask to seek advice from I was on my own.

His marijuana smoking had increased to the point of constant use when he was not working, and it seemed to allow his volatility to ebb somewhat. His finances were a mess and his spending had escalated to the point of withdrawing money from the bank daily. Money was an issue between us because my pay was more than his and he was spending more than he was making. His stance was he had gotten me the job I had so whatever money I made was his. Our marriage was something I wanted no part of. His high sexual demand and his coarse ways were detrimental to anything I might remotely relate to love, it was more reminiscent of hate to me. Deciding I wanted to leave was a decision slow in coming though because I went through a spell of thinking maybe I could do things well enough to placate him, but nothing I done helped. As a matter of fact, it made him act worse. One day I cleaned the kitchen floor. Washing and waxing it which I done weekly. He came into the kitchen, made himself a bologna sandwich with mustard on it and I could feel the hostility coming off him. He began yelling at me for some perceived infraction, it was always something. Taking his sandwich and throwing it against the wall he said, "I'll give you something to clean up, since that's all you want to do." Without any type of reaction, I went about the business of cleaning up the mess. There was nothing else to do. Fighting was not an option and murder was not either. It seemed my gender elicited from him emotions he was unable to handle. My willingness to please him and refusing to fight caused even more anger to arise in him.

It was during this time that I forgot to get my birth control prescription filled. Thinking I would wait a month and do it, is how I received one of my greatest blessings ever. Becoming pregnant, I continued to work. This pregnancy was totally different than my previous one. No morning sickness at all, which was a blessing because had it been like before I would have had to quit my job. My thought was maybe this happening would cause my husband to treat us better. It didn't, he began demanding more than ever before, asking repeatedly who the baby belonged to because it wasn't his. Especially if it was a girl, he would know it wasn't, all he had was boys. Since I worked second shift, I always cooked lunch before going to work when he was home. His shift changed monthly, so when we worked the same shift, or he was on night shift he demanded I cook. One such time I was about eight months pregnant and was cleaning the dishes after eating. He began a tirade. Grabbing me he ripped my maternity top open exposing my stomach. Crying, I simply went into the bedroom, changed clothes and went to work.

The following week he went to day shift and on my way to work, we met at the entrance to the subdivision where we lived. Pulling over to visit a minute before continuing on my way, he pulled over as well and got in my car. Immediately I saw I was in trouble. Grabbing me by the throat, he took his revolver, pulled back the hammer, put it to the side of my head threatening my very life, which was also threatening the child I carried in my belly. Fearfully I assured him of my never-ending love for him. Calming, after assuring me he would kill me, I continued to work my shift. Thankful that he would be asleep when I got off work because he had to work the following day.

Telling my supervisor, I was pregnant, and would need time off to give birth, he stated he had nothing to do with my being pregnant, could give me two weeks off before my due date and two weeks after the birth since there was nothing in our union contract to deal with pregnancy. Thankful for any time at all to be with my children without Warren being there was a blessing.

Awaking at three o'clock in the morning of December 8, 1975, I thought I had peed the bed. With my other birth my water had never broken so I knew nothing of such a thing. That's what it was, it had broken. Getting out of bed, I called the doctor. Telling me to wait until nine o'clock to go to the hospital, Warren popped some popcorn while I washed the sheets and put them back on the bed. Eating the popcorn, my rear molar on the left side was cracked from the car wreck I had been in and the rear of it came off. Calling the dentist's office, I made an appointment to have it taken care of on my way to the hospital. Labor pains had not started. My amniotic fluid was still leaking out, on my way to the dentist appointment, so I folded a dish towel to a thickness to absorb it and put it in my underwear.

On arrival, they told me they would have to induce labor because my baby wasn't wanting to come, and I was having what was called a dry birth. However they induce labor, they did that to me, taking me into a room with another person who was in labor as well. They would come to check me periodically and monitor my progress. Simply moaning when the pain came, the nurse asked me why I wasn't screaming like the other girl was doing, I just told her it wasn't hurting that bad. Again Mrs. Wheatley was right, I was built for having babies, just like my mama.

Warren came to see us and with one look at my baby girl it was obvious who she belonged to. We both were evident in her. She had a cleft chin like her dad and plump cheeks like me. She was beautiful. Weighing a whopping six pounds, ten ounces, just a few ounces less than her brother. I was so pleased and happy until her dad looked at her, then looked at me and said, "who does this thing belong to?" If it was a joke, I didn't get it and I made my mind up right then and there we were through.

Enjoying and reveling in having both my babies with me even if it was only for two weeks is a feeling I'll never forget. Not wanting to return to work I knew I had to because my life depended on it. Naming her was again as with Gary, never discussed with the father. Feeling total responsibility for it I again searched my mind for a suitable name. At the time there was a girl who had overdosed on drugs by the name of Emma Ann, and this was all over the news. Hearing the name so often, it was in my head, so when I was asked what I wanted to name her, that is the name I gave. I would like to say I gave it much thought and came up with the name after much consideration, but that is not the case. After all, the things I was dealing with were life threatening events and I was internalizing all of it as a fault of my own when it was just the plight of women at the time. My husband would taunt me with saying, "who are you going to call, the police, no one cares about you?" Knowing my vulnerability, I had to choose to keep my mouth shut or suffer the consequences. I would still lull myself into thinking perhaps we could make it but then an eruption would happen again. If it had only been me, I maybe could stand it, but seeing my son abused was more than I could stand.

That summer the union contract at my work came up for renewal and we went on strike to have our needs met. Unconcerned about the contract, the best part for me was I got to stay home with my kids. It was only a couple weeks before it was over, and we went back to work. During this time my relationship with Warren had not improved and some of the things he was doing I knew were wrong.

Anything causing me happiness, such as Gary coming to live with us caused him to create more dissension. My daughters' birth, even though she came from him, was something I was not allowed to show any happiness over. All my happiness must come from him and only him, but there was none there. People know when they misstep and cross lines it's just that they feel they have you in a spot and can act, be or do any manner of atrocity to you with no repercussions. Repercussions exist though and not at the hands of others. It is simply the Law of Cause and Effect, and we all have these laws to live by. Leaving him was not something I wanted to do but seemingly it was forced on me.

Warren had a long-ago friendship with a man who had assisted in getting him his first car when he was seventeen. The man's name was Wendall. He and his wife had recently moved back to town. This man had gotten in touch with Warren because he needed some help. Warren invited him and his family out to the house for a visit one Saturday when we were both off work. This man had a court date coming up and needed a favor from my husband. These were the days before computers and information traveled much slower. He wanted Warren to testify on his behalf concerning the theft of some heavy equipment he was involved in. This would require Warren to perjure himself on the witness stand and I was against it because of our family. Talking to him about it resulted in his telling me this man was his friend and he was going to do it as a favor to him. Telling him he should be paid at least if he was going to swear to a lie caused more anger to be directed to me. It seemed there was nothing this man and I could agree on. His physical good looks that had attracted me to him in the first place became a vision of ugliness when he would grab me by my throat and with a distorted grimace of his features tell me all the horrible things I was, with spittle flying, teeth bared venom radiating from him like heat from a stove. Knowing I had to make a move, not wanting to, once more, I attempted a conversation about his behavior. The eruption never happened when I told him how this was making me feel, it always came afterward, when he had time to process my words and decide I was being disrespectful to him. At one point I was told my tongue needed to be cut out. Another time I would stand in front of the door and have my say. Fearing losing his job, he wouldn't chase me outside when I would say what I needed to and then leave. Knowing if he chased me a neighbor would call the police, his reply was, "bitch, you can't outrun a bullet". Having a hard time accepting someone could be so mean to me, made it more difficult to leave. Pure hell at that time was my life.

Finally, we concluded we needed to separate. Warren helped me find an apartment. Moving in with my children, it was a relief to come home from work and not be subjected to all the abuse. My sister Cheryl was babysitting for me at the time. She lived in a neighboring county, and it was a half hour drive to take the kids to her in the mornings and retrieve them in the afternoon. Fear and loneliness are companions I had at the time, and they were not favorable ones. They got the best of me, and I called Warren. I didn't know anyone, and being twenty-two years old, it was taxing on me, so I reached out to the only person I knew, and it was him. My family was judgmental and blaming. I hate to say it but it's true. Along with the poverty of my upbringing and the patriarchal teaching I was a classic example of exactly what was happening to me. As people used to say, "no brag, just fact". I needed help with everything. From childcare to money to mere existence. Sounds like excuses but it's the truth. Warren and I began seeing each other again. He decided to sell the house and move into the apartment with me. We began going to church to try making a go of it. I was of the Morman faith, having been baptized as a youngster, so we began to attend a church nearby. We would have the missionaries in our home to eat with us and pray. This seemed to anger Warren even more. His attempt to manage himself was such an effort that he could not maintain it. On one occasion we went to K mart and Gary wandered off as children will do. Finding him he snatched him up and spanked him right there in the store. If that had been the end of it and we could have gone on with our evening all would have been okay, but his tirade had begun and continued. We stopped for a gallon of milk at a convenience store and upon arrival at the apartment Gary knew at four years old to go to his room. As he was rounding the doorway into the room, Warren hurled the gallon of milk at him, hitting the wall at the end of the hallway. Shattering all over the place, it was another job for me to clean up before going to bed, along with listening to his ranting and raving. Again, this was a repeat of what our life together was like. I could not do things well enough, nor allow enough of anything to get along with him. Somehow, we concluded we would get marriage counseling which seems crazy now because I think by this time we were divorced. It's hard to track this period of life because living with such chaos causes the mind to not function well. We began seeing a counselor in the spring of 1977. Things seemed to be better for me because after a session with her, I was able to vent and speak the things I had held in. He seemed more receptive to monitoring himself to control his eruptions of anger. My tolerance level was at an all-time low as far as allowing my children to be abused and I do think he was trying; however, he could not be something he wasn't and could not maintain himself to do what was needed. Having a blow up during a session the counselor told us she would only see us separately, while during the session, when I got through speaking, she asked Warren to state his feelings about what I'd said. He was becoming very agitated in his body movements, and it was obvious to her he was getting ready to explode. I felt safe having a third party there to say what was on my mind concerning a fight we had had earlier in the week when he had overreacted to the children. His reply was on point when he told her, "One thing for sure, if we were home, she wouldn't be saying that." He was right I wouldn't say anything because I had learned to keep the volatility down as much as I could at home.

He moved in with his brother. We both began seeing other people. I didn't want a relationship with anyone, I was just lonely and when Eddie took Gary for the weekend and Warren took Emma, I had time on my hands I didn't know what to do with. I began going to a club, with a woman I worked with. She was an alcoholic and was jealous of me. Not knowing how jealousy presented itself, I thought she was a friend. One Friday at work we made plans to meet at the club to dance and have fun. Long story short she didn't show up, so I went ahead and sat at the bar having a drink. Not knowing why I was there it wasn't long before someone let me know why they were there, and I hung out with the manager of the band that was playing that week. He was from North Carolina he said and had been a lineman before becoming a band manager. We left together and went to the motel where they were staying. Spending the night with him was awful. I did not enjoy our sex at all. He was a big man, over six feet tall. Insisting we shower together we did. Then he began pawing my body and was very rough. Next morning early, before he was awake, I got up and left, driving to my apartment, I felt sick to my stomach. Vowing to never do anything like that again, I did not realize the power of alcohol or the power of fear and loneliness. Both these are entities that can supersede the best of intentions causing not only me but anyone to behave in ways that are completely alien to us.

Thus began my summer. Warren needed some furniture, so he came to the apartment on a Saturday to get the bedroom set. I cannot remember how it came about but we began arguing. He hit me, knocking me across the table into the wall. His brother was with him. I am so thankful he was otherwise I would have been beaten to death that day. Once I was on the floor, he was on top of me beating my head with his fists. His brother got him off me. Picking up my purse that contained my .22 pistol I went outside and sat on the steps leading from the parking lot into the apartment, thinking I would shoot him if he accosted me again. He did not.

We continued to be in contact because I didn't want what was happening in my life to be happening, so we held onto the nothing we had with each other. I'm sure his life was better with me in it, and I needed help with childcare and all aspects of life because I didn't know women could live alone. I didn't know anyone who did and the things I experienced living by myself were not what I wanted, so I continued to hope things would get better. Since I made good money that came into play in his decision to ask me to get an apartment upstate when my lease was up in the fall of 1977. I assented. Living there was closer to my work, and we seemed to get along better but he had begun to "act out" at work. Even though he wasn't blowing up as much with me, he began to think he was a vigilante and could stake out people's houses on his off days. There was rape of older women going on in the south end of the city where we lived at the time, and that was all he could talk about. He had his brother go on a stakeout with him to try to arrest this person who was doing the rapes. His workplace had him hospitalized to do a mental evaluation and he wound up being told to resign or be fired. He resigned. Wanting, rather knowing I needed to get away from him, I moved from the apartment to a rental trailer nearer Cheryl. Getting close to my sister so I would have childcare so I could work. The place I rented was not suitable for us. Suffering from all I'd been through, I still believed in wanting to do all I could to have my relationship with him work. My upbringing and my vow to myself to be a good person thought I needed to maintain a relationship with a man. That's the best I can come up with as to why I continued to see him, but I did. Along with the rigors of work, childcare, and home maintenance my mind was in turmoil. Unable to love and care for my family the way that was needed as well as my sex drive caused me to allow him to visit me, and consequently I became pregnant with my third child.

He had rented a trailer in the neighboring state and asked me to visit with the children. I did. It was a good visit, as he was displaying charm and hospitality. This caused me to think maybe we could make it when he proposed to me. He was working in construction, hanging drywall. The money he was making was enough to take care of a family living the way we were, with no aspirations of being anything more than paying bills on time and eating regularly. Saying all the things I wanted and needed to hear, I assented. According to his thinking it was my working with mostly men causing our troubles, so I gave up my job and moved in. We remarried. Coming back to the trailer after the ceremony, I went to the bathroom, and he followed me in there. Grabbing me by my head, jerking me up off the seat he began berating me. Telling me how stupid I was to believe what I was told. Realizing immediately my mistake in thinking he would be any different than before, the following Monday I returned to my work to try talking to them about getting my job back, but they didn't want anything to do with me.

What a disappointment. One of the reasons I had returned was my son had started school and I needed help getting him there and back as well as having a toddler it was overwhelming. Warren continued working so while he was at work, I was able to collect myself enough to function. Still not knowing I was pregnant, when I skipped my period and told him, he stated I had to have an abortion. We had to go to the inner city to get it. Ads were in the paper advertising the cost and address of where to go. It was on Jefferson Street, in an old, converted house on the second floor. There were sixteen beds in there and all of them were occupied. Mostly teenagers. Speaking with one girl in particular who was in the bed next to mine, she was sixteen years old, and this was her fourth abortion, she said. I was in shock. Unable to comprehend the mess I was in. No blame, just actualities of an existence I could not understand. The cost was five hundred dollars. I was two months pregnant. I didn't tell anyone about this until years later when the full scope of all that had been came home to me. As is said "the chickens always come home to roost".

The company he was working for took a job north of where we were living and it would require him to be gone all week, only coming home on Friday and returning Monday morning. He and a coworker were going to ride together. I was looking forward to him being gone because he was toxic to be around, and I wasn't allowed to show love for my children when he was home. He left for work, and we were preparing to go to the pool when there was a knock on the door. Answering, there he stood. Asking why he was there he stated he believed it was a set up for the police to lock him up. Not explaining why and I knew better than to ask questions, the pool outing was canceled, and I had to spend my day in the bedroom comforting him and telling him everything would be ok. Leaving the children in the living room watching television.

Constant turmoil was my life, with the only thing keeping me together being my children. That was my normalcy and it seemed it was his consternation. He went to bed and stayed there for weeks. Once he healed a little, he decided he was going to enroll in classes for coal mine restoration. Without a place to go, we rented a U-Haul and retrieving our furniture from his brother's house we drove to the town where the classes were being offered. I drove the U-Haul and he followed me in the car with the children. Caught in this maze of his craziness caused a whirlwind effect on me and there was no way to escape. When we arrived, we drove around and saw an empty house sitting near the road. Nearby was another house and he went up and knocked on the door. A man answered and Warren asked him who owned the empty house, the man replied he did. Asking how much to rent it the man told him an amount and we rented it. Going in this place was again an experience I could make nothing out of. It had four rooms, no indoor plumbing, the best I can say was it didn't leak because it started to rain. Unloading our stuff, we had to make a trip to town to buy food and get a hotplate because we didn't have a stove. After making us something to eat, we went to bed. Putting Gary on one end of the couch and Emma on the other end, we went to sleep. This trying to be a good wife and honor my husband was proving to be a thing that seemed too hard for me to do.

Warren began classes at the community college there, and I began a job at Jerrys restaurant as a waitress. There was no way we could exist here, and I told him as much. He decided we would return to the trailer where we had been, since we still had it rented. On arriving back neither of us had employment and I was nearing the end of my patience with him. His sister lived in town and rather than finding a job he decided for us to move in with her, her, husband and three kids. All this was going against the grain of how I wanted my life to go. Going to the unemployment office to get help finding a job, I was able to get a job at a company as an inspector. We made parts for telephones and electronics. This place paid five dollars an hour. The year was 1977, so this amount translates to around twenty-three dollars in today's money.

Since I detested living with people, I immediately began a search for an apartment. Finding one I could manage on my earnings meant we could not be too selective because supporting all of us didn't leave too much to play with. I found a two-bedroom one bath apartment on Railroad Street, across the tracks and it really was across the railroad tracks. The rent was one hundred fifty dollars a month. When we looked at it, Warren stated, "I cannot live in this place". My reply was, "I'll make it look nice, just wait and see". So, we went on and rented it. Working at night from eleven to seven in the morning, I would leave work, go to the apartment, clean and decorate for our moving in. I did make the place attractive for what it was. It was on the second floor, the steps leading up to the entry door and the walls were filthy, so I washed them. The people living across the hall had a little boy, and she stayed home while her husband worked, so I asked her if she would babysit. We agreed on a price of 40 $ a week. She allowed my children to sleep there for that amount. Warren got a job with a beer distribution company, so we had more money to work with, but it wasn't too long before he made a delivery to a restaurant and left the doors on the back of the truck open when he took off, consequently spilling his load of beer in the middle of the street. I had just got off work and had taken Gary to school, sitting at the table I heard a key in the lock and my heart sank when he entered the living room and told me he'd been fired. Keeping me up all day there was no way I could go to work that evening. He was losing his mind, but I didn't know it. His behavior became more and more bizarre. Deciding he wanted to go to White Castle at the same time we took lunch at my work, we went, and I saw several coworkers there who went back and told my supervisor. Returning to work the following night she asked me about it, and I told her exactly what had happened. I was through trying to cover for him. Still not knowing what to do I told him he had to get another job. Applying to the city police department they hired him. Before he was to start, the very night before he was to begin the next day, he said they really wanted him to work undercover and he was going out to begin a shift of undercover work. This made no sense to me, but I didn't say anything to that effect because I couldn't stand to talk to him. He called his brother to go with him and they left. He wanted to take Gary, but I was able to convince him it wasn't a good idea because he needed to go to school. I just wanted him to leave and get away from us. Consequently, he didn't get the job, rather was picked up by the police and returned to the State Hospital.

Knowing I needed to make more money, I was constantly looking at the help wanted ads. A steel mill in Little Rock had an ad for a quality inspector so I called to inquire about it. The human resource manager told me on the phone that I needed to get my equivalency diploma, since I had dropped out of high school. The library at that time gave GED testing in one day. The test was four hours long, so I went and took it. Calling back to set up the interview, I was hired. Warren had been released from the hospital, so he was able to keep my children. I worked the second shift. My pay nearly doubled, going to nine dollars and fifty cents an hour. This afforded us a better standard of living, so he began looking for a more suitable place, more up to his standards I would say. I had made friends where we lived on Railroad Street and other than all the trouble with Warren, I was happy.

Moving to Top Line Apartments on State Street was a step up. There was a pool, and the area was better. The people living there earned more money than where we came from, the cars were nicer but really the quality of people is the quality of people. There is good and bad anywhere you go, and this was the case here. Our immediate neighbors were drug dealers and they got busted. One day I look out the patio door and see a man running up the hill with a pistol in his hand. Following him was a police officer. That was the end of them. The apartment became vacant and I'm glad because after supper one night I'm cleaning up and I hear a gun blast. With the history I had with Warren and his numerous declarations or threats that he would kill himself or me, I thought he was making good on one of them. Entering the dining area, Emma is sitting at the table still finishing her dinner. Gary was standing midway between the living and dining area with the shotgun in his hand. Warren had been cleaning it before we ate and had laid it down on the sofa. He entered from the hallway, attacking Gary, he fell on top of him and began beating him about the torso area. Yelling for him to get off my son, he came to his senses and let him up. We were all dazed by this. I'm sure we were in shock. Sending the children outside to play, of all things I took him to the bedroom to calm him down. Not daring chastisement for leaving a loaded gun out, with children in the house, he was incoherent. After calming him, I brought the kids back in and called the police to make a report because it had to be done. Gary was scared he was going to jail, and he was only seven years old. Making a report, I'm unsure what their true thoughts were surrounding the situation. Probably the same as mine, because who does that? I was an adult, but he was the one watching the kids while I cooked. Not making an excuse, rather the fact of the situation. Having him there was like having another child. The only difference being he could do great damage to all of us and was doing exactly that. Overwhelmed is an understatement, we were all on edge. There was no depending on him to act in an adult manner.

After the police left, he said he needed to go for a drive to clear his head. I was glad to have him gone. Calling Cheryl, I told her what happened and asked if we could go there. She said yes, so collecting a change of clothes for us all we started to the car. Gary said, "here comes dad". Asking me about what I thought I was doing, he ushered us back into the apartment. Instructing the kids to stay outside and play, he and I continued inside. Once the door was closed, he attacked me. Grabbing my arm and slinging me against the wall demanding I love him and never leave him. Placing himself between me and the door, the assault continued, all the while I am pleading with him to stop. Finally suggesting we go get ice cream. Agreeing with me, that is what we did. My arm had a bruise on it from the shoulder down to the elbow, so he got a long sleeve shirt for me to put on even though it was summer. After getting the ice cream he wanted to not return home but to go to visit my family. On the way we had the car windows down on the 1974 Thunderbird we were driving. They were automatic and the driver could control all four of the windows. Gary was leaning forward in the backseat letting the air hit his face. All at once he began screaming. Warren had rolled the window up and Garys ear was caught between it and the frame. Did he do any of this on purpose? I cannot say he did, but to me it seemed as if all these things were calculated events.

Arriving at my brothers' home, of course they were happy to have us. We spent the night. Next morning my sister-in-law made a big country breakfast consisting of eggs, bacon, sausage, gravy and biscuits. She put all the food on the table in bowls and platters. Gathering around the table, we all passed the food around to fill our plates. When the egg platter had been passed to everyone there were a half dozen eggs left on it. Warren took the platter and emptied the remainder of the eggs onto his plate and ate them. Getting up from the table he went outside behind the house and threw up everything he had eaten. Not coming back into the house, he continued walking up the hill behind the house into the woods.

Waiting most of the afternoon for him to return, when he didn't, I told my sister-in-law we probably needed to call the sheriff's office and report it. She made the call. Responding to our call, they informed us someone had called in about a man naked in a field of mown hay, asking us to come to the location and see if it was him. We went to the road indicated and sure enough there was Warren in the field, stark naked, picking up handfuls of straw to cover his privates. They handcuffed him and put him in the back of the police car. Coming to me they informed me they were taking him to Lee County Hospital for an evaluation. Unable to handle the situation, they transported him to a better equipped hospital in the next county. I followed the ambulance to the hospital. Going into the emergency room where they had him in a strait jacket and subdued, he said "that is not my wife, I do not know who that woman is". I was past all emotions or feelings of any kind, I was numb. Taking my leave I returned to my brother's house, retrieved my children and returned home, relieved to have some peace. Driving back to our apartment was a three-hour drive. It was nighttime when we got home, but we all slept peacefully.

The resulting fallout from this resulted in him once more being transported to the State Hospital. I had been laid off from my job at the steel mill and was drawing unemployment at the time, so the kids and I had a fun loving few months. It was summer and we went to the pool each day. We didn't have much money, but we could pay the rent and eat, our needs were met. We went to the hospital to visit Warren weekly. Eventually they put him on lithium and got him what they called stabilized, and he was able to come home. The time he was away was liberating to me. My neighbor was a friend and she done all she could to assist me emotionally. Inviting me out with her and her estranged husband to a club in the city. He paid for our dinner and drinks, then suggested we meet again the following week to play golf and have dinner, she became jealous and said we needed to leave. Accompanying her because I was riding with her, she assured me that she wasn't mad at me, she was mad at him. Going to the bathroom before we left a man approached me and asked me for my phone number. Crazy enough I gave it to him. When I got home, I paid the sitter and she left. Before going to bed my phone rang. It was the man. I was drinking and lonely, so I gave him directions to my home. The kids were asleep. He was driving from the club, and it was a good thirty-minute drive from there to my house, but he came, and I let him in. We had sex. It was horrible. All I needed was attention from someone not what we engaged in. Putting it out of my mind, I simply forgot about it. He didn't, and he began calling me. I told him I was married, and my husband was coming home, which was the truth. This man was trying to make me his girlfriend. That was not what I wanted, telling me about his house and pool and all the things he thought a woman might be interested in. All I wanted was for my husband to be a husband to me and stop doing all the crazy things he kept doing. When Warren came home from the hospital, we continued as before. He gained quite a bit of weight taking the lithium, but the mood swings and physical attacks lessened.

Wendall had stayed in touch with Warren throughout the years by phone. He would call occasionally to chat and see how he was doing. He phoned one Saturday and invited us to visit him and his family. Warren idolized the man. Driving out there, the home they lived in was very nice. We visited and they were wonderful hosts. Warren and Wendall decided to go run around, leaving me and the children there with his wife and kids. They were gone for hours, into the evening. I didn't understand that way of doing. Asking his wife where they were and how she put up with it she said she used to get mad and fuss at him for staying out like that, but she decided to accept it as long as he kept the money coming in. I never found out where they went or what they were doing. Returning, it was late, and the kids were already asleep, so Wendall wanted us to spend the night, so we did.

At this point my unemployment was running out and the unemployment office sent me to American Standard to interview for a job, as a casting inspector. They hired me. This was the era of affirmative action of the seventies when it was mandated companies hire minorities who had been discriminated against because of race or gender. My job consisted of standing in what they called the sanding booth where the bathtubs made of cast iron came down the line on tracks, with a piece of chalk in my hand, marking the chunks of metal the finish grinder needed to remove before applying the enamel. It was dirty, nasty work. With all the personal protective equipment I had to wear it would have been extremely hot, but it was March, so it hadn't gotten hot yet. My hours were three a.m. to three p.m., I hated it. I could have done it had the pay been well, but it wasn't. After working there for about three weeks, Wendall called Warren and invited us out for a visit. We went and during our visit he asked where I was working. Telling him he said, "you should come work for me". "Doing what?", I asked. "Dancing" he replied. I said, "I don't know how to dance", he replied, "you don't have to know how, just circulate and have fun". He had gotten a club out of town on a busy highway. It had girls dancing and hustling drinks. He wanted us to go out there, since it was Sunday, the place was closed so we drove out to see it. All of us went, kids and all. Loosening up with a few beers, I got on the stage and sort of walked around. Music will get in your body and cause movement if you have any rhythm and allow it to flow through the body. There was no pay only commission on sales of cocktails. I'd never heard of anything like that before, since I was naïve in all respects. He said I could make five hundred dollars a week, which seemed like a small fortune to me. Warren wasn't working at the time. He was getting his allotment from the military to go to school. I said I didn't think it would work for me and I had a job. He said give it a try, for one night. Agreeing, when I went to work Monday, I told my supervisor at American Standard my grandmother had passed away and I needed to be out of town for a few days. I didn't feel this was wrong because my grandparents on both sides had passed long ago. My career as a dancer, hustler, whatever anyone chooses to call it, began on a Wednesday evening in 1980.

The clubs' hours were from six o'clock in the evening until two in the morning. Drinks were five dollars for the small one. The way it was set up was to sell sixty cocktails to earn two hundred dollars and after that you got half of whatever was sold. All tips were yours to keep. The first evening I worked I sold fifteen cocktails. We were not required to drink alcohol, and I didn't at first. Since I had such a long drive home, I was scared to drink.

After the first night working there, I returned to American Standard, cleaned out my locker, threw my coveralls, steel toed shoes, hardhat and whatever else was in there, in the garbage can on my way out the door. It seemed a good move for me because the nature of Warren, there was no depending on him, and I didn't know how to get public assistance. The only time I had ever tried was when I lived on Railroad Street, working at the components factory. They told me I made too much money and had a car. Feeling I had to rely on myself to care for my children, I took full responsibility for it.

One of our neighbors had kids my kids played with. She and I talked at the pool. A knock on the door one morning was the little boy, sent down by his dad, to tell Warren he needed to talk to him. She and I had become close enough to speak about the troubles with our husbands. Her husband worked for a steel company out of Chicago. They knew Warren was unemployed and I had begun working at a club. He went down to speak with this man and the guy offered him an opportunity. It was a good one too. A job with pay enough for a family to live on with only one person working. It consisted of routing incoming steel bars to various companies in the metro area. Thirty-five thousand a year was the starting rate. His workplace was a train yard with a construction trailer sitting on it with a computer in there sending the bar description along with the destination on a tag, attached with a wire. Located right off interstate, I would stop to visit him on my way to work at the club.

Warren had difficulty staying in the reality of our life and the responsibilities associated with being a parent. I'm thinking we were on our way to having all we needed as a family, and he was thinking something totally different. One such visit, on my way to work, he had spent his free time composing an introductory letter he wanted me to present to people that bought me cocktails stating for five thousand dollars, they could buy me for the weekend. I took the letter assuring him I would do just that. Hurt, disappointed, and realizing nothing had changed, I could tell the mania was back. Somehow, I knew we couldn't ever have a livable existence. When I left his office, he was elated by the prospect of me doing what he had requested, while I tore the letter to shreds, throwing it out the window of my car, tearfully going on to work with my stomach churning. By this time, I had learned the signs associated with the disease he had and knew within I couldn't make a life with him, if I was to have a life, I had to make a life for myself. Maybe that's how it is anyway, but why have a husband if that was how they were going to act? Still, I didn't want to be three times divorced with my children to raise by myself. All the negative emotions imaginable I was feeling but I had not been taught about honoring my emotions or feelings, only to be a wife and mother and the sins I had committed already haunted me with guilt to the point of not realizing I deserved to be treated well. If this was the energy I was releasing to cause him to behave this way, why did other people like me and spend money to talk to me? Why was it that the one I wanted to create with asked me to do these unspeakable things and put me in danger? It hurt me yet caused me to think less of myself. Being a normal person with a normal existence was all I wanted to be, but it wasn't happening. I wasn't angry, I was hurt.

Only working at this place for a week, when he asked me if I gave the letter to anyone, I told him the truth. Angrily he told me I was dumber than a box of rocks and I needed to do what he said if we were going to make it. He said there was no use in us working all the time when we didn't have to because I could make enough money and we could stay home with the kids. I'm listening to all this unable to process what I'm hearing. He was so emotionally possessed by his thoughts that my not speaking was not even realized by him. Demanding we take a walk; we walked up to the end of the apartment complex. Pointing out cars with out of state license tags, he told me we were being watched and these people were there to kill us. I'm in a trance listening to all this and trying to assuage him enough to prevent him from more hysteria than he was already experiencing. Having no choice but to leave the kids with him that Friday evening I went to work. When I returned the next morning after working until two a.m. he was gone. On the table in the dining area there was a letter written on toilet paper, stating that he would not return and take care of the children. His son was living with us at the time, so I had three children to find a sitter for before going to work that evening. Calling his ex-wife, I told her the situation and she came to get her son. A sixteen-year-old lived in the apartment below me so she agreed to come to my apartment and be with my kids so I could go to work that evening. Even though his leaving presented a hardship for me I was relieved he was gone. His actions had caused me so much distress I felt I could deal with anything I oversaw. My biggest issue was childcare.

Relieved and temporarily eased emotionally with having a sitter nearby, gave me some time to figure out what I needed to do. His timing was well thought out because it was the end of the month and rent was due. Paying by check, knowing the funds were there because I had been depositing the money I earned, I was surprised when my check was returned for insufficient funds. The lease was in his name, and I could have stayed there and made them put me out, but I didn't know the rules surrounding things like that besides I considered myself an honest person. Having a grace period on payment I went to work and made the money in three days to keep us housed. Knowing I needed to move closer to work I lived there another month before I gave notice that I was moving. Still not knowing how society viewed people who done what I was doing for a living, I was in for a rude awakening when I began looking for a place to live. To tell the truth, I found out is not always the best option. I had to lie to get a place. I had to get someone who was coming in to see me to pose as my husband and rent the place in his name, and I would pay the rent. I explained the situation to him, but he thought something else. He thought we were going to be married and began telling people that. When I confronted him, he got mad at me. Having already told him my reasons for needing the favor it really came down to the money, who would pay the rent, but he seemed to not understand that. The place wasn't even sufficient for me. It was one bedroom and I needed at least two bedrooms because of the children, but after giving notice where I lived, I had to move.

Contacting my sister Cheryl, we decided she would allow the kids to come stay with her until I could find a place to accommodate us. Paying her one hundred dollars a week, she stepped up and helped me. It was not what I wanted but I needed to work, and it was all I could come up with. Not ideal but I could see them on Sunday, because I worked six days a week. Unable to foresee the challenges I would face I was attempting to solve my personal problems one at a time as they arose. Overwhelming is when the things one is facing become insurmountable. I had not reached that point yet. It was a relief to know where my kids were, and I figured they knew I would take care of them. Never considering nor explaining to them what was happening I now can understand the fear and abandonment they must've felt. At the time I had become inured to the harshness of life and expected nothing else from it or people. They say you get what you expect and that is a true statement. My takeaway from my experiences thus far was people will like you if you do what they want you to do, and if not, they can be cruel.

Part Three ——————

Working at the club was fun. Totally immersing myself in the atmosphere and relating to the people in a way that found the commonalities between us causing me to be a popular addition to the place. Twenty-seven years old at the time, I was starting this career at a late date, as nearly all the women who worked in this industry began much younger. Most of the time in their teen years. I was not liked by my co-workers. There is much jealousy and evil thinking because of the easy access to all manner of vices. Alcohol, drugs and base thinking can breed the adverse conditions associated with hatred and criminal behavior. Not knowing this, my caring nature echoed to the customers as well as the women I worked with. True to the nature of things, I began to find out people will not always treat you as you treat them.

One man, who frequented the club took a liking to me and decided I was exactly what he needed to further his life plan. I was not in the market for a relationship, but he was helpful to me in ways that caused me to incorporate him into my life. When I had moved to the one-bedroom apartment he had been indispensable in my move because the person who was supposed to help me bailed. Duncan Farnsley was his name, and he came into the club daily. He was thirty-six years old, which to me seemed ancient. In my naivety, I gave no thought to any why's or wherefores of anything. Dunk as I chose to call this person, became a huge part of my life. We began an on again off again relationship. He was a construction worker by trade, but didn't work for a company, rather took jobs on his own and hired help as needed. Working just enough to get by and selling caffeine pills he bought at a head shop to drug addicts in the clubs up and down the strip. He had targeted me, and I was clueless. Always there to pick up any slack in my life he was an alcoholic and drug addict himself, but he knew the streets. Schooling me in ways no person in my life ever had before. Taking the time to give me care and advice that worked when needed. I grew to love him. Not romantically, rather as a person like a family member. Taking our relationship further than occasionally hooking up and taking him home with me after work, was not something I wanted. He wanted to get married. The picture he painted for me was a pretty one and he was kind to my kids, endearing himself to me in all ways except I was not ready for commitment after what I had been through with Warren. Trauma is something that needs to be processed and personal responsibility for allowing such treatment to happen to oneself, understood before moving into another situation. I didn't know this with words, only intuitively, unable to explain to him anything other than I was not wife material at that time. My first obligation was taking care of my children, not even realizing that I was neglecting them by removing myself from them physically. Physical need was all I was aware of at this point in my life. Acknowledging emotional need and tending to it was something I was not able to do. On my own and refusing anything other than letting out my frustration and pain with inconsolable crying when it got the best of me. Suffering was all I knew how to do. Respecting me for the dedication I had for taking care of my family, yet at times fussing at me because of my refusal to get public assistance, we did have differing views concerning women and their place in society. Having been to his house, when he offered, rather asked me to move in with him when initially I was hard pressed to find a place to live, I knew I couldn't live there. The place was unkempt, not large enough nor the kind of place I saw myself living.

I began drinking whiskey and thank goodness I never developed a taste for it. Drowning one's sorrow is something people say but it never worked for me. Drinking made it worse. Blaming Dunk is not what I want to do here, he had demons worse than mine, again I didn't realize anyone had any pain except me though. Always being there for me was his penance because I treated him badly. There I said it, but he never took it personally because he saw the good in me and knew it wasn't personal to him but a reflection of my feelings toward myself, along with my life experiences thus far. Still believing I was unworthy of love, his display of affection to me, I could only interpret negatively. Having tried to depend on a man and let down in every way possible I was immune to the part of myself capable of loving another romantically. He would give me ultimatums. Either I agreed to marry him, or he couldn't see me anymore. Laughing I would tell him I loved him but didn't want to get married. Sometimes he would get angry, but he never hit me or called me names, just tried pointing out the futility of what I was doing even though I was continually seeking employment in other areas. Following through with his threat to stop seeing me, he stopped coming into the club.

Since my work was from early evening to early morning, I was able to job search during the day. Also, I had picked up some bad habits from the environment I was in. Dealing with people as closely as I did, it was inevitable that relationships would develop. Learning how far others will go to get what they want, how deserving they feel, and the callousness and justifications offered to themselves for uncensored behavior. With Dunk out of my life and my children living with my sister I lost my identity temporarily and became the alter ego my job required of me. Going by the moniker Barbie, so named by the wife of the owner of the club when I first debuted on the bar scene, because she said I looked like a Barbie doll, I morphed into a new personality. Among the clients who came in to talk to me one man stands out. He was in real estate and took a liking to me. His business brought him out past the club, and he stopped in one day, this is how we met. Wanting to see me outside the club, I was skittish because I was fearful of what could happen. My need exceeded my fear though because he knew of my circumstance of having two children and not enough room at my apartment to have them with me. Sharing my wants and needs was one of the things endearing me to people taking the time to get to know me. Not everyone had the means to afford the time to do so. This man was married, with a family. Most of the people coming into the club were. Telling me he had a house for sale he wanted to show me, I agreed to go with him to view the property. He said I could buy it on contract. He was enthralled with me, and I liked him okay and the arrangement was better for me because he couldn't hound me about getting married because he was married. We rode around together drinking and visiting different properties he was involved with. Going to look at the house, it was a better fit for me than where I was living. It consisted of three bedrooms and two bathrooms. Needing some work, I could live there cheaper than the apartment I was renting. School was still going on, so my children were still at my sister's house. Wanting them to finish out the year so they wouldn't be disrupted again, I went ahead, broke my lease and moved in. Initially I had roommates because I was somewhat fearful about buying. Renting a room to two of my coworkers, my cost would be less than a hundred dollars a month to live there. They had phone lines run to their bedrooms for privacy reasons, but everyone had kitchen privileges. We all worked six days a week anyway, so we weren't home that much. Only on Sunday and that's when my children visited. It was not ideal and lasted only until school was out. These were honest but transient people, and I didn't feel bad about asking them to move. By the time I asked them to move they were ready to go. One of the girls got married to a G.I., the other one moved to a pay by the week motel. The man's wife had gotten wise to his antics, and it was causing him trouble, I guess. Really not wanting him around the house, he only came there a couple times before I had to tell him I couldn't have him there.

One day on my way to work, I was walking across the parking lot and someone at the traffic light, which was red, called out to me. It was Dunk. He turned around and pulled into the lot to chat. Asking me how I had been we had some conversation, and he began coming in again. Telling him about the house he said he could help me with it since he was a carpenter/ builder. Not wanting to get involved with him again I declined the offer. He knew exactly where it was located, since he had lived in the area for twenty plus years. I needed some help but still wasn't ready for what he wanted and knew it would turn back into what it had been before.

One morning around nine o'clock I heard a scraping noise outside my bedroom window. Getting up, going to the front door, looking out there is Dunk on a ladder scraping the trim and overhang on the eaves of the house in preparation for painting. Asking him what he was doing he replied, he was prepping for paint. Saying I needed help and didn't have enough sense to know it, I probably should have run him off, but I didn't because he was kind of like a stray dog. That is how he presented himself to me. He climbed down and I asked him in for coffee, and it began all over again. Knowing how he felt toward me and knowing how I felt toward him I knew it was a doomed relationship from the get-go because he thought he could change me, and I saw him for what he was and couldn't accept it. He was at the time the only friend I had. My workplace had become toxic. Wendall had gotten in some trouble and needed money for a lawyer, so he said he had gotten robbed of all our pay and all the dancers who got paid out weekly didn't get paid. I had enough savings so I could stay afloat but after not being paid everyone left except for me. He hired some goons to come in to run the place. Going to work one evening one of the guys was sitting at a table with a long gun on his lap with a bar towel over it. Things were getting really tense and uneasy. I had a call on the pay phone, and it was Dunk. Telling him what was going on he told me to wait a certain amount of time, then come out to my car and he would meet me there. Doing as he asked when I went out the back door, true to his word he was standing by the side of my car. Leaving and driving to my house he said he thought I should quit, so I never went back. Shortly after, Wendall was sentenced to a term in prison, and the place closed.

Not knowing how I would get by because my kids were coming back it seemed as if my world was falling apart. Once more he became the knight in shining armor, telling me to go downtown to the food stamp office and apply for assistance. After my previous experience in trying to get help, I thought I'd be turned down, but he said I needed to pay more attention to my appearance when applying. Telling me to not comb my hair nor dress nicely, rather wear baggy jeans and oversized sweatshirt because if I was clean and put together, I would be turned down. I did need help but didn't know the ins and outs of getting it. Learning the truth of a saying my mother always said, "the truth is not always the best way to go". Attempts to tell the truth cannot always bring the results we want or need. Without any income, and the job market in the early 80's being a time of scarce employment opportunities, I needed some help and didn't know anything about getting it. Doing as he said, it worked, and I began to receive help from the government. Having been raised as I had listening to my dad speak ill of people receiving assistance, I diligently pursued employment.

Applying for a job at a car dealership near my home, there was an on-the-spot interview. The man taking my application said wait because the hiring manager wanted to talk to me. Thinking this was a lucky day for me it was a surprise when a short stocky man entered the room with my application in hand and sat on the edge of the desk near the chair I was sitting on. Very friendly, he began by telling me he was interested in me coming there to work but was interested in my work history. Once more telling the truth seemed to not be the best avenue to take. He said, "I see where you were working at a club as a dancer". Replying, "yes I was", he continued, "were you the owners girlfriend?" "No," I said. At this point is when he propositioned me. Stating he had statewide connections with people and could set me up with men to make some good money. Not knowing how to respond, I stalled and told him I needed to think about it. Shocked with his words as well as apprehensive because he had my address and phone number. That night I was awakened by a phone call. It was late, eleven o'clock or so. Startled and groggy from sleep, I answered, the man on the line identified himself as the person who I had the interview with. Asking me to meet him at the dealership to talk further about a job. I told him to never call my number again and hung up the phone. Astounded by the brazenness and audacity of this person I sought out my confidante Dunk. His advice was getting the man on tape it he continued to call me. I didn't have to do that because I never heard from him again.

Finally, school was out, and I was able to bring my children home. This was a glorious day for me. They were happy as well. We were a family again. Dunk continued to come around and they loved him being there because of his good nature. It was healing for all of us to be together and he wanted once more to integrate himself into our life. Running him off, both Emma and Gary would get mad at me and act out accordingly. He played it to the hilt too. It seemed everything was stacked against me. My babysitter for them lived across the street from me, which was convenient, but she was an alcoholic as well as her two grown sons who lived with her and didn't work. I found out from another neighbor that my children played out in the street with no supervision. All this was cause for me to allow Dunk to move in with me and consequently begin running my life. Wearing me down to the point where I agreed to marry him. Since we had the same last name already, even though he and Warren were not related, it was easy to just go to Tennessee and get married by a justice of the peace.

It was okay at first, but his addiction to his way of living began to show itself not long after we were married, when one evening he didn't come home from work. While I was cooking supper Gary was sitting at the table and said, "mom, where is Dunk?". "I don't know," I said. "Do you think he has another woman?", he asked, I replied again, "I don't know". This wasn't the kind of life I wanted at all. Feeling the vulnerability of my position, when he finally came home the next day, I told him how I felt. He said he had told me that he had many weaknesses and he had. I just didn't know what that meant. My thoughts were, decide to do something and do it, not make a promise per marriage vows and then systematically go about breaking them. Getting over being angry with him, and making up, I decided I wanted to go back to work, he suggested a small club up near town. This place was in the lounge of a motel where usually there will be a band playing, but there were dancers rather than a band. It was small, maybe a dozen tables along with seating at the bar. We would usually have as many dancers. Melanie was the name of the bartender. She was a short blonde who had been in the business for a while. Dating the owner of the club who was married, she carried herself as a "toughie" but was good to me. She wanted to be closer than I did. I maintained my distance from the others because I was different. I was not looking for a man to take care of me I was looking to get by, take care of my family and that was it. Even though Dunk and I had gotten married I had difficulty accepting the fact of where I was and what I was doing. It didn't jive with my thinking of what a family should look like.

Working here, I began realizing that the same people I was seeing while working at the previous club were coming in here. That's what I realized as creating a following. Dunk was conducting an experiment

I believe to see how much of a draw I was. After watching what had happened at the club once I had come to work there, he had a long-term plan to realize his dream of ownership of a bar and I was an integral part of the plan. He decided I needed to move down to the farthest end of the highway to a club called The Nougat Lounge. It was larger, closer to an army base and my prospect was better for earnings. The man who owned it had several clubs downtown. The women working there were different. The lady running the place was named Marilyn. She seemed okay with me. My main objective was to get along with everyone and make enough money to take care of my family. I had stopped my government assistance when Dunk and I married. He made good money when he worked. He was in the club most evenings for a drink, then went home to be with the kids. Working from Wednesday through Saturday my life was pretty settled at the time. We got along and he was nice to be around. He liked gambling on a regular basis. He always had an account at the Downs, a racetrack where they raced trotters. Betting nightly from home, somehow it could be done through hooking it up with a bank account. Not thinking anything about it I didn't have an opinion either way about his gambling or how much he spent if we could pay the bills and get by.

Jealousy was rampant in the business I was in, and girls were always attempting to put a bluff in on me to not talk to people they called their customers. My way of thinking was I would speak to whoever came in and inquire how they were, how they had been etc., irrespective of who they were sitting with. This caused a girl to confront me in the dressing room one evening. Telling me some man I spoke to belonged to her and I was not to speak to him again, I simply stated my reason for being there was to make money to take care of my family and I would suggest she do the same. She never acted like that again to me.

Dunk began to talk about opening a club with me. There was a building sitting empty that had been a club in the past. Owned by a man Dunk spoke of who had lost his business due to his alcoholism. His manner of introduction of the idea was ownership of a club would afford us the ability to never have to work again. Failure to consider the fact that I enjoyed my job or perhaps he did take it into account, because ownership requires the ability to work when no one else wants to. As is said "the path to hell is paved with good intentions" comes to mind here though. My belief is he did have good intentions or rather neither of us had anything to lose. It would either work or not. His presentation to me was, "would you like a club of your own?" I said yes because it was the next logical step to making more money. He saw in me the ability to manage the things he was unable to do.

Before I agreed to marry him, he had to finalize his divorce from his previous wife. The house he lived in was the conundrum. He would not agree to the finalization, because it was in both of their names, staying there without upkeep or even paying the utilities. Many times, during the time of first meeting him his electricity would be cut off or his water would be shut off. He would come to my apartment to shower and stay until I had to ask him to leave. He was a player on female sympathies and kindnesses. These tendencies were among my reasons for not wanting to get married to him. Once I agreed to marry him, he tied up the loose ends of selling the house and splitting the money with her. Since he didn't have a bank account, he gave his proceeds to me to put in my account along with his last paycheck from a job he had recently finished. Knowing he could trust me because of my trustworthiness. These actions caused me to believe that he was sincere.

Once I had agreed to work with him on opening a place, he set about finding out whatever information we needed to initiate the process. Mornings were free because I worked at night and only four days a week. Driving down to the empty building we gained entrance by removing a piece of plywood covering an opening where a window unit air conditioner had been. Standing at the bar with my leg stretched out, propped up on it to stretch my hamstrings while he was checking how much work was required to get the place opened, someone behind me said, "what are you doing in here?" It was the County police. Startled I called Dunk to come. Confidently, he talked with them, telling them our intent and what we were doing. They told us we needed to get permission from the owner to look at the building. Having already found out that the owner of the building was in a nursing home and her lawyer was handling her estate, we had contacted him, and he had told us we could look at the building and see if we could do anything with it. Dunk told the officers this. Satisfied with the explanation, they left us alone to look around.

Continuing to work at the Nougat, we would work during the day while the kids were at school to ready the building to open. To make an application for a beer license an address had to be named so we leased the building contingent on license approval. It took three months for the process to be completed so in the interim we were able to get things ready. We began in February, so it was spring before we opened.

The manager where I worked had gotten wind that I was working during the day at the building up the road. Asking me my intent, I told her our plans. Not knowing how others react, I never thought anything of it. Dunk had asked me at first not to say anything of our plans, so I didn't but by the time she asked me about it there was no way to deny I was working during the day up there because my car was there. Having told only a few people that came in to see me about our plans, somehow, she began to think I was stealing her customers. That's what she said at least when she fired me. Unconcerned about the firing because I knew people were going to go where they wanted and stealing anyone was not my intention, it hurt my feelings once more to be falsely accused.

Dunk had taken a job remodeling Jerry's restaurant. Since they remained open during the remodeling he worked at night. This job afforded me the opportunity to work on the building while he slept, and the kids were at school as well as enough money to keep ourselves afloat while waiting for everything to come together. Life was good even though I missed working, I stayed busy. Dunk and I went out often. When he wasn't working, we went to the bars and often would have too much to drink. I still trusted him, even though our relationship was not what I considered conventional. We had fun and he was the kindest person I'd ever known other than my mother. His kindness reminded me of my mother, and that's how I loved him. He knew this because I was truthful with him about how things were for me, but I was faithful because I knew the pain associated with adultery and didn't want to experience that again. Never identifying characteristics I needed in a mate, only identifying the things I needed to do and when I failed in that respect, I was unrelenting in my self-chastisement. He was willing to give to get what he wanted, and it wasn't me, for me, but what I could make happen for him. That's the fact of the matter for both of us. We were in the same place, seeking safety from the storms of life in one another. It was convenient to marry him since I didn't have to change my name. our last names were the same already.

We progressed. He had two daughters, one from his first marriage and the other from a long-term relationship he'd had with a woman a few years older than me. It was mostly sexual, he said. The oldest girl was seventeen when we married. She lived with a man Dunk done business with at times. This man was older than Dunk. They would come to visit and stay in a motel while in town. At my suggestion they began staying at my house when they were in town. Never meddling in his affairs, I was clueless about the things he was involved in. I trusted him completely. Whatever he wanted us to do I went along without a fuss.

Opening day came and he was ecstatic, while I was terrified. He and I were the only workers there. We had a Derby party since it was Derby Day. This was to become a tradition for us in the following years. Opening at noon, the place was slow starting off, but by early evening it was full. I was running myself ragged trying to take care of all the customers. He was drinking but I wasn't because I was too busy. Between dancing on stage, waiting tables and helping him bartend there was no time. We had a fruitful first day in business.

Closing time was two a.m. and by that time I was ready to go home. We had already locked the doors after having last call, when a knock alerted us that someone was at the door. It was a friend of Dunk's and his wife. Dunk allowed them to come in and instructed me to bring everyone a beer. I did. Exhausted, all I wanted to do was go home because we had to be back at noon the next day, but I went along with what he wanted because he was my husband, not knowing any other way. He always made me feel secure in whatever we decided to do.

Setting up a meeting with a man to help us with our bookkeeping, we met at a bar to speak with him. Years later he told me his thoughts concerning our decision to open a bar. Stating, here's this little couple putting their life saving into opening this place and they're going to lose their ass. Determination is a word few people recognize when seen in action along with recognizing opportunity as well as "striking while the iron is hot". When there is no other option on something working, it will work. After meeting with this man, he told me what he needed from me monthly and we set up a plan of working together. We became friends by association. Seeing the receipts from our first month in business, he called and asked Dunk about going in business together. We met at a restaurant one Saturday morning. He was manic from excitement, stating he wanted to set up a corporation with us. The cost to incorporate was five hundred dollars, Dunk said write a check. Never asked my opinion about it, I just did as I was told. The corporation never materialized other than on paper. He was excited about the money we were making and wanted to be more a part of it than a bookkeeper. My husband revealed to me that he didn't like the man, but at the time he was just someone to help with the business. I didn't give a thought either way about like or dislike.

Taking on the role of sole proprietorship, this thing had to work, there were no two ways about it. Dunk's ex-sister-in-law contacted him about a job. We needed a bartender, so we hired her. Some of the girls I had worked with in the past began coming in or calling and this is how we were able to get positions filled. It wasn't long before we had a full crew. Trust between mates is a good honorable thing, but blind trust can be fatal, and I did have absolute trust in my husband and his leadership abilities. Alcohol and drugs can and do take down many and the residue of their usage began to come to the forefront. I began drinking and using pills and marijuana. He frowned on my marijuana use but I ignored his words. It seemed the crowd we were a part of everyone done something. His thing was pills. He never had a prescription, rather obtained them in other ways. I never bought marijuana because the people who came into the club gave it to me. At this point in my existence, drug abuse was a part of life for everyone I was in contact with. It is said alcohol and drugs, but I say drugs because alcohol is a drug. My drive was strong and coming from a life of lack, my only motive was work. Putting in long hours, I took the lead as far as making sure everything ran in a timely fashion. Things became a blur for me. Working more than being at home, my days began at noon and ended sixteen hours later. Just to get up and do it again. Thoughts of childcare other than them needing anything from me other than housing and feeding was a foreign concept to me. Putting so much energy into the business, I had little left for anything else. Dunk expected me to be there, and I followed through. It only had a beer license but even the die-hard liquor drinkers would succumb to drinking beer, just to be there. It became the place to go. These things get noticed because other bar owners are always checking the parking lot to see where the cars are.

Learning human nature and the ability to read through actions and behavior is a multi-faceted talent I did not possess at this time in my life. Believing that people act in their best interests I was yet to learn a major lesson in how far they will go to take revenge on a life partner. One such lesson came from a customer that had just retired from his job. He began frequenting our club every day. Being enamored with me he requested a drink be sent to me and asked for my company. Sitting with this person became a full-time requirement. He was there when we opened and stayed until closing. Each time I needed a refill he asked if there was a more expensive drink he could buy. Relating to me how much money he had on him and that he wanted to spend it all. One evening we were watching the show, and he clutched his chest and fell off the chair onto the floor. He was having a heart attack. Calling an ambulance, he was taken to the hospital. Having open heart surgery, the first thing he done when released from the hospital was begin coming in the club again. He had stopped drinking and smoking. Asking me to marry him I began to suspect he was crazy because he knew I was married to Dunk. His wife began following him and had hired a private investigator to follow him to find out what he was doing. Asking him why he was spending all this money he told me it was his and he could do as he pleased with it. He said he and his wife had planned to sell their home when he retired, buy a Winnebago and travel but his youngest daughter was getting a divorce and had moved back home with her two small sons and the wife had allowed this to happen. He didn't like the arrangement and that was his reason for frequenting the club and spending all the money. I began attempting to distance myself from the situation because I sensed danger.

One nightclub down the road from us was called Marvins club. So called because that was the owner's name. It was a popular place during the seventies. It had live bands and dancing. He visited Dunk one evening and they went to the office and talked. Later, on our way home, I was informed that Marvin had offered him a business proposition. He wanted us to go in business together and change his venue to dancing girls. It seemed the bikers had made his club a hangout causing people to not want to frequent the place. We had been at our current location a little over a year. Deciding we would work out a deal with him and create another club. We, along with Marvin took a trip out of town to visit a club that only had a beer license, the girls didn't sell cocktails, rather danced for tips. If a customer liked a particular girl, he or she could buy the girl a drink, but the girls didn't work on commission, they just worked for tips. This is a better arrangement because it puts more distance between the girls and customers, making it easier to maintain one's aura. Buying one of the girls a drink we told her we were there scouting talent. She and her boyfriend lived in a motel nearby. Arranging a time to meet her there the following day, we left the club. The following morning, we went to the motel and talked with her further. She was twenty-four years old and seemed eager to make a change. Marvin owned his building and it had furnished apartments on the second floor and one in the rear of the building. Telling her we could offer her a place to live as well as be the star of the show seemed to resonate well with her. Of course, the boyfriend had to come. The plan was in motion. We told her we would call her when we had the club ready for opening. She and her man came when we notified her we were open. She served the purpose of a new face, which was the main reason for her, but she had other ideas, of course I don't know what Dunk had told her in private. Becoming jealous of me, she got drunk one evening and threw a fit saying she was better than this, whatever this was I never knew, and she and her fella left the next day.

This place took off like wildfire. I was still at the club up the street but would meet with Marvin every Monday morning to go over the week's receipts. His wife took care of all his bookkeeping and filing quarterly statements.

We decided to take a break for a while and go camping with the kids. We took them all and went to a campground. Sleeping in a tent together we laughed, told funny stories and had an all-around good time. Arriving home the next day, late in the evening we got a phone call from a man who owned a restaurant across the road from the club, it was on fire. Devastated, we drove down to see all we had worked for, go up in flames. It was a total loss. The girls who worked there were out of a job. When the news got around my phone began to ring wanting to know what we were going to do. Telling them not to worry we would figure something out; I didn't know what I was going to do either. I had become so used to working there, I didn't want to go down the road to the other place. It was bigger and the atmosphere different. There was no other choice though. Beginning to work down there in the daytime afforded me more time to be at home but it would be short lived.

Marvin had been in the bar business for many years. Revealing to me some of his history, he had the first go-go bar in that area. He changed to live bands and dancing when he had married, as his wife didn't approve. Since Dunk and I had partnered with him we oversaw the dancers, his involvement was minimal and acceptable for her. Marvin was sixty years old, just waiting for the time so he could retire. He came down to the club each morning but rarely came in at night. Short of stature, he wore three-inch heels on his shoes, dyed his hair black and told everyone he was forty-nine years old. Relating to him the story of the man who had spent so much money at the place up the road, he asked me the man's name, telling him he began laughing and said it was a neighbor of his that borrowed his lawn mower to cut his grass.

Dunk decided I needed to tell Marvin I wanted a quarter more commission on drinks I sold as well as all my tips. Doing as he asked, Marvin refused because he said we were in a three-way partnership, and I was getting a third of the profit anyway. It wouldn't be fair to him if I got more commission. When I told Dunk his answer, he then instructed me to inquire about the far side of the building where Marvin had operated a restaurant at one time. Ask him how much he would rent the place to us for. The place was long and narrow, but it did have two rest rooms, which is required for public places. Marvin said we could rent it for three hundred dollars a month. It had to be constructed into a bar because it was just an empty space, but with Dunk's skills as a carpenter, we rented it and began constructing a bar space. Applying for a beer license the time frame to open was three months. We began working on its creation. Once the thing was constructed, I cleaned the space, and we were in business.

Calling it by the same name of the business that had burned, I came from next door, as well as all the girls that had worked with me. Even though we only had beer because the law stated an establishment needed to be a certain number of yards from another establishment serving liquor, business took off.

Business began to fall off when we left and one Monday when I met with Marvin, he told me his decision not to give me another quarter commission on drinks was the worse decision he ever made. Laughing, we remained friends even though he accused me of taking all the girls with me. I reminded him people can choose where they want to work and who they want to work with. It became an ongoing thing between us. He was from the age of men being more authoritative and telling women what to do so credit given for the abilities to converse and entertain were not admitted.

Our businesses thrived until things began to change. Change is a funny thing. It'll creep up unannounced and cause an altering of circumstance all the while seemingly remaining the same. Dunk had an affinity for drug usage and was forever the opportunist, while I was only interested in moving toward property ownership to enable myself to not need to work so much. The next logical step to my way of thinking would be buying the property and leasing it to someone else. We could not get on the same page with our thinking. Meanwhile his criticism of me and my parenting/work habits as well as not doing exactly as he said without offering up my ideas, caused him to dive deeper into his addictions. Without any knowledge of the way addictions present, things seemed clear to me, and I began to experience emotions I had never felt before. His answer was to keep leasing bars and my workload became nearly unbearable. Telling him how I felt fell on deaf ears. Another bar came up for sale. Not the building but rather the business. It was the same building as the club Wendall had owned. Someone else had it leased, and Dunk had set up a meeting to buy the business from him. The amount we paid was twenty-five thousand dollars, with an amount in cash, then a contract for the remainder. The rent on the building was six hundred dollars a month, and five-hundred-dollar payment on the business for two years. Dunk had invited his brother to enter into the agreement by asking him to use a portion of his retirement fund from the factory where he worked, to become a partner with us in the corporation we formed. He agreed to the arrangement. I still was acting as a puppet for my husband even though I was not agreeing with his tactics. We had grown apart. His drug usage was taking over his life, but I was clueless since I worked so much and never questioned his comings and goings. He had invested in the purchase of a couple of racehorses we were paying to stable, at a farm. Dunk had things structured according to his liking, but my workload was overwhelming. When I attempted to speak to him of my concerns, he began avoiding me. He and Marvin decided to close and revamp the largest place and change it to a disco, with a D.J, catering to the black crowd since there was no place that had done so at that end of the highway. We hired a D.J., to work there three nights a week. Charging a cover at the door, that's what we depended on to pay for the help and stay open. People would pay the cover charge, bring their own bottle in and buy a coke so we were mostly selling cokes and maybe some beer. We weren't making any money. Marvin didn't really care since he had already made all the money he needed to make. Dunk was riding high on his ego, not caring one way or the other as long as e could maintain his status of whatever it was, he was trying to portray. I'm going nuts trying to stay up with all that was happening. There was no talking to him. Still going along with his schemes, it was too much when he bought a herd of horses and was asking me to pay the trainer, boarding bill as well as veterinary, hay, and all expenses associated with such an enterprise. Speaking with my husband about such matters never produced a change. Finally, I told him I wasn't going to continue paying these outrageous bills because there was too much money going out and nothing coming in except the money from the clubs. After taking over the last club we had bought there were weeks that the tiny place I was running was paying to keep all the places open. Anger set in on both sides of our relationship. He felt I owed him, and I felt overworked, overwhelmed and disenfranchised. I had voluntarily slowed my workload down. Staying home more. Marvin called me on a Saturday midday and told me I needed to go get Dunk. He was in the parking lot of a liquor store passed out, his truck door open, legs hanging out the door. Driving down to the store, there he was, exactly as Marvin had said. It was ridiculous. Arousing him I got him in my car, and the man who ran the liquor store came out and gave me a brown paper bag full of cash he said Dunk had on him. Stating he had taken it inside because he was afraid someone would rob him. Dunk didn't want to go home, he wanted to get a room at a motel, saying he didn't want the kids to see him like that. I went along with him because I didn't want it either.

His oldest daughter had come to live with us since she was ending her relationship with the man she'd been with since the early teen years, so I didn't have to be concerned about the kids being at home alone. We got a room at a motel, and he wanted something to eat. I walked to MacDonalds to get food and after eating he fell asleep. Sleeping for hours, when he awoke, he began calling me names and telling me how worthless I was. Telling me he had made me and acting totally out of character. Still not recognizing nor understanding how addiction affects people I wanted to make things better, but this was the beginning of a long arduous journey of disentanglement leading to many changes I had to make to get away from a way of life I didn't understand. He told me he was going down and was taking everyone he knew with him. Nothing he said made any sense to me. The next morning, we went home but nothing was ever the same again. So began the systematic behavior to take me down. Unable to focus on work, not caring about anything other than the loss of my relationship with my husband, I stopped going to work and began trying to monitor his actions and behavior which was futile. Remembering all the times he had wanted me to stay home or calling me to come home after working my shift, but staying because either I was busy or had too much to drink and wasn't ready to leave. Self-chastisement and misery were my constant companion. Accepting all blame and fault for what was happening, I was the perfect pawn. Not understanding how people will use you as justification for their own errors and shortcomings, I was the perfect person to blame. Not wanting to leave the house because I was afraid I would miss his call, I sequestered myself. Still responsible for paying the bills at the small club I ran; I decided I had to distance myself from him. When he called me, I set up a meeting with him to come by the house and I met him in the driveway. Giving him the checkbook with a healthy balance in the account and all the bills paid, I told him I wanted a divorce, and I was leaving my position. I wanted ownership of the last club we had purchased since I was listed as president anyway. Thinking in my naivety he would honor my request since it seemed he didn't want to be part of my life anymore, was not how things panned out. The person we were renting from was from was a criminal defense lawyer in Little Rock. His group housed the best defense attorneys in the metro area. They were the ones you wanted to get if you got in trouble. He didn't take cases anymore but could advise. Contacting him about a divorce, he said his office could do it, but he could not because it would be a conflict of interest. Telling him to go on and put it on the docket I later called and told him to take it off when my husband came back home and convinced me otherwise. Not really wanting a divorce, rather wanting him to discuss our situation with me, understand where we were and conceive a plan of action to plug up the holes, I was indecisive. Dunk knew this and was playing my emotions to the hilt. Calling the lawyer for the third time to set the divorce, he said, "Are you going to do this or not?", you're making a fool out of yourself". Angered, I replied, "go on and put it on the docket, I'm going through with it".

It felt good to make the decision and stick with it. Attempting to serve papers on Dunk proved the next obstacle. Seemed he was determined to make things as difficult for me as possible. Every time the sheriff's office sent someone to serve him at the club where he hung out after the disco went bottoms up, the bartender said he wasn't there, even though he had simply gone into the office and closed the door. The sheriff's office was not concerned with tracking him down and he knew that. After several attempts to serve him they called and told me they couldn't keep it up, I needed to tell them how we were going to get this done. Telling them I would set up a meeting the following Saturday at a hole in the wall bar up the road. "How will we know who you are" they asked. "I'll be wearing a red dress", I replied. This cat and mouse game we were playing was getting old and embarrassing for me, it had to stop. Hanging up the phone I immediately called the club, asking to speak to Dunk, he answered since the game he was playing was so much fun for him.

That isn't a snide comment, they really were. He felt he had me. Since I had always up to this point been a dutiful wife, he either believed we would continue or simply could not face the reality of what was happening. The place where we were to meet opened at noon, and I entered shortly after they unlocked the doors. Ordering a draft beer, I chose a table in the center of the room so as to be conspicuous. Having processed the realization that, I could not continue in my marriage with the drugs and the people he was hanging around, our lives had gone down the tubes. When he came in, he had a cap on the back of his head, and he never wore a cap. His gait was even different. Walking springingly, he had always walked slowly and methodically, I was disgusted with him and his appearance. Going to the bar he got a beer and joined me at the table. We were the only people there. Making small talk for a few minutes, such as the how are you's and I'm fines etc., the door opened, a large man in uniform walked in, came to the table, threw a folded paper down in front of him and said, "you've been served", turned and left. As soon as he approached our table, I got up and walked out, hearing a string of cursing as I went. Not knowing how the event was going to be received, I wanted to be sure someone was there, not that they could do anything, but I needed to make it to my car safely. Pulling out of the parking lot I headed home, with him right behind me. Emma had spent the night at one of her friends' houses so there was no one at my home, and I didn't want to go there. Unsure of what his intentions were, I drove into a different neighborhood, with him still tailing me. He had hit me once before and knocked me out, but it was justifiable because I was yelling and screaming at him after I realized he had robbed me of the cash we had been saving. He had always presented a kind caring nature, but as of late his demeanor and all-around appearance had changed to someone I did not recognize. Scared, not knowing what to do, all at once I thought how silly the whole thing was. Pulling into a driveway, I turned around, and went to my house. Following me, when we got there, I went to Emma's room, and he came in there as well. I had laid down on the bed, he came in and raped me. After it was over, he got up and left. Giving into my emotions, I wept until I couldn't cry anymore, got up and went on with my day.

I had tried to stay with him and didn't want what was happening to be happening. I had tried the cocaine, even going as far as hanging out with him and the people from The Liquor store, where they had set up a drive through to sell cocaine. One Saturday they were waiting for a shipment to come in and I was there in the back room with all of them. There were a couple of girls there that had worked at the club. They were all skinny and had a glaze in their eyes. When the delivery came, they started cooking the stuff in a test tube mixed with a liquid. They were making crack, but I didn't know it, I was just trying to hang out with my husband. Taking the rock that formed after the cooking, they put it in a pipe and smoked it. It stunk. Smelled like burning rubber, like tires smell when set on fire. After this experience, Dunk and I left and went to a pizza parlor, drank beer and shot pool all day long. Once I realized this was the way of life he was choosing it scared me because I didn't like the way I felt the whole time. I only wanted to be with my husband, but this was not the person I thought he was, he had hoodwinked me to get me in his trap. Having wondered when we first met why a man his age was living as he was, he knew exactly what a woman needed from a man to worm his way into her life. It's difficult to admit even now, how far I went to try to maintain my marriage. The dissolution had to happen, or I would not be here telling the story. He had an emotional hold on me that I misidentified as love.

He didn't show up for the divorce hearing, so I was granted what I had asked for. Inheriting his brother as a partner since he was named on the corporation as an acting member, we were still attached through him. So many things still lay in store for me to learn, the ways of myself and others perception as well as societal rules is not any easier for a man than a woman and early life experiences are oft times repeated until the lesson is learned. Feeling as if a milestone had been reached, he continued harassing not only me but his brother and daughter as well since we were partners, and his daughter was a bartender there. He came in at night and asking his brother to talk to him and tell him not to come in, I was simply told, "that's my brother". Unacceptable answer, but I had to accept it. He used the fact of being her dad to manipulate her into giving him a cash "draw" of three hundred dollars. When I saw this the next day, I spoke with her about it and she said she didn't think about it one way or the other, since she was so used to us being married. Telling her it had to be paid, she assented. There was no other way to recoup the money other than taking it out of her pay, a little each week, until the debt was satisfied.

Ending each year, I began thinking about how I wanted the upcoming year to unfold. 1989 was the beginning of this habit. Acknowledging the fact that changes had to take place, even though not to my liking, my divorce became final on January 13th of that year, which was a Friday. Celebrating, an associate and I went out drinking at my club the next evening, which was a Saturday. Business was slow that evening. Sitting at the bar a man and his girlfriend came in who were regulars. He began chatting us up, his girlfriend became jealous, when he slid his keys down the bar to her and she stormed out the door. He left before we did. We continued sitting at the bar talking with the bartender. When we decided to leave, I was driving my car and hadn't locked the door. Opening the door there the man was laying down in the backseat. Sitting up he said, "I'm going with you all". I told him we had to go get his girlfriend, it wasn't right the way he had treated her. Giving us directions to where they lived, I sat in the car while he and the person I was with went inside to get her. She refused to come with us, so I was satisfied we had done the right thing. All we were doing was going to my home. Once we arrived, we continued drinking until we ran out of beer. I wanted to go to sleep, but not with him there. I told him I would take him home.

He didn't want the night to end even though it had already ended because the sun was coming up. Under the guise of obtaining more booze he suggested we visit a friend of his who would have some. Attempting to pacify him we went to a location off the main road to a double wide mobile home where I blew the horn on the car and a man stuck his head out the door. Saying he didn't have anything to drink, I realized this person just wanted to show off that he was in the car with me, so on leaving we took him back to his house, went home and slept.

Life after my divorce from Dunk was the same except, I did ask him to stay away from me and he did. He did not stop the stealing and aggravation in any way he could. Finding out my habits was easy because my routine had not changed. I was working less but the times when I picked up the money from the closers was the same and he knew that. Using this knowledge, it was easy to set me up for a burglary, which is exactly what happened. Meeting on a Wednesday with the nighttime bartender to pick up the receipts of the previous days the sum was a hefty amount. Dunk had been in the club when I entered and immediately left. Going into the office the bartender followed handing me the bank bag with the money and register printouts. It was early evening, just getting dark. Leaving, I went home. Opening the back door going into the kitchen, I was grabbed from behind by a man with a mask over his eyes, with eye holes. I never saw his face only heard his voice say, "throw your purse out the door, bitch" while pushing me into the kitchen. Then he said, "put your purse on the kitchen counter". I replied, "do you want me to put it on the counter or throw it out the door?". "Throw it out the door". Doing as instructed he pushed me onto the floor and ran. Hearing a loud engine start up, the getaway car had been sitting at the dead-end street in front of my house. My children were in the house asleep. Picking up the wall phone in the kitchen, it was dead. The phone lines had been cut. These were the low life people I was dealing with. I had a roll of quarters in the glove compartment of the car and still had my car keys in my hand. Driving to a convenience store nearby I phoned the police to make a report, but nothing came of it. I never found out who robbed me, but the remnants of the incident reared its ugly head once more later.

I had to get a new driver's license and replace whatever else that had been in my purse. This incident occurred late winter. Early spring my phone rang, and it was a person who lived a few streets over from me saying they had been doing some yard work and found my purse in the hedges in the front yard of their house. I immediately went to get it. It was sodden from being out in the weather, but everything was there except for my driver's license. No problem since I'd already gotten new ones, I didn't give it a second thought. This was part of the long game to take me down though.

Dunk had been setting me up for a long time. Before our divorce I had come home one day and there were books of personal checks scattered around the back door of my house. He was with me because it was one of the times I still hadn't accepted it was over for us. He was seeing how far he could push me. He said he thought Emma had been playing with them and had done it. Accepting his explanation, I picked them up and sorted through them, realizing some were missing, I reported them to the bank, and they assured me they would put a watch on the numbers that were missing. He knew it was only a matter of time before I would put him out and this was part of his preparation. When I had done exactly that, he needed my driver's license to use them. This did not come to light for me until a year later when I called the bank, which I done occasionally to get the last five paid checks. This was a service they had started to assist in keeping tabs on one's account. Being late in the evening the bank was closed, so when the check numbers the recording gave me were out of sequence with my checkbook, it took a second before I realized the numbers given were the checks I had reported missing the year before, the ones they were supposed to be watching for. Waiting until the bank opened the following day, I was there when they opened. They were able to tell me all the checks were written the day before at area Kroger stores, in the total amount of fifteen hundred dollars. Deducing that he had sat on the checks for that long of a time and then having someone rob me was a harsh realization and at the same time helped me to realize further that I was doing the right thing by putting him out of my life. Since there was liability on the bank from my having reported the checks missing as well as Kroger for letting them pass, I was set up with the head of security at Kroger headquarters located in the east end of town. During the interview I swore I had been robbed, that I had reported my checks missing, had renewed my driver's license etc. all the things I had done and had happened. There were records of all these things, so the money was restored to my account and Kroger had to absorb the loss. Happy to get the incident behind me and have it end the way it did eased some of the trauma of the incidents that led up to it.

Being a young woman I still had sexual urges and working with men it was only natural I would be attracted to someone, and I was. I had an attraction to someone representative of something totally different than anything I had experienced before in my life. Working closely and conversing intimately with him, after my divorce I felt free to date anyone I chose if I kept it away from my workplace. I wanted a mate, but not the drama I had with my marriages. Thinking it was none of anyone's business what I did in my free time and needing an escape from the stress of running the business I embarked on a relationship with a person I had met in the club two years prior by the name of Noah Jameson. He was tall, dark, and handsome. There was an attraction from the first time we had met for me. He was married but separated. Working in sales he was charming and honest to a point. His honesty consisted of just not talking about his marriage, rather allowing me to think what I thought which was, he was divorced. Family oriented, he was a responsible person, taking care of the needs of his elderly parents as well as his children. None of the men in my life up to this point had done this. His second job brought him out to the area of the highway where my business was located, and he came in daily. I gave him my phone number. He wasted no time calling me. It felt good to be wanted enough to be called and chat with someone who acted like they wanted to talk to you rather than having clinkers thrown in front of you. It touched a part of my heart that had been dead for a long time.

We met for the first time outside the club to go to dinner one evening at the parking lot of a Holiday Inn. Not even considering I was followed or that Dunk would be concerned about my movement or activity it was a good date. Going to Red Lobster to eat, then driving around the city before deciding I didn't want to go home, I told him as much. Escaping from the hostility and all manner of atrocities I had been experiencing, I wanted the feeling to last. We got a room at a motel across the river. Staying the night we consummated our relationship. Driving back the next morning to pick up my car, he circled the lot to my vehicle. Getting out of his car, and approaching mine, he pulled out of the lot and left. Unlocking my car door, I was attacked from behind. It was Dunk. Knocking me down onto the seat of my car he began scratching my face. Yelling for him to stop, he came to his senses and did stop, but not before both sides of my face were covered with nail scratches. He left, so I waited until he had time to get gone before I left to go home. My mental state was incomprehensible. Why would anyone act like this? Not wanting to be with you and yet not wanting you to move on. My decision to divorce him was a long, painful time in coming with detrimental behavior and neglect of myself and my life to appease him, so the culmination of the unfolding of events was accepted by me, but he still thought we would continue as before. It began to seem Dunk knew all my moves before I made them, but I gave myself away by my openness. The club where he hung out and owned had a bartender that Noah had talked with about our first date and eating at Red Lobster. When Dunk asked me how the food was at Red

Lobster it planted the seed even further that he was psychic. This man knew the rules of psychological manipulation to a T.

Contacting my landlord, asking him if he would sell me the property my club was standing on, we came to an agreement that he would sell to me on contract with a ten thousand dollar down payment, setting it up on however many years I wanted. Consulting my partner, to see if he wanted to do this, he said he was agreeable with the deal on however many years I wanted to go for, so I set it up on a five-year contract. We went from paying six hundred a month rent to paying fifteen hundred a month payment. This amount wasn't scary, I knew we could do it from having had to pay five hundred a month on the business along with the rent. That debt had been satisfied, so the business was paid for, the next logical step was purchase of the property. Seemed everything was going my way. My workload was slowing down, and I felt I was finally seeing some light at the end of the tunnel.

No such luck though. Dunk continued to harass and make trouble for me. I say me because it was up to me to remedy anything that happened. Going in to clean the bar one morning, there was a table that had been moved into the stock room with a bottle of Jack Daniels sitting on it along with two empty glasses. Entrance had been gained through the roof. rather than seeing this as a way to secure the place and plug up holes to prevent things like this from happening, I allowed myself to get angry, causing me to feel helpless. It began to rain later that day and the entire roof began leaking. Almost as if holes had been punched in random spots on the roof. Sitting buckets and various containers around to catch the rainwater, I went home totally exasperated.

Noah knew someone who did repair work, so I called the man and met with him to get an estimate on the cost of a new roof. The building was old, at least a hundred years old according to my landlord. There was an opening in the eave that allowed someone to use a ladder and gain entrance through the roof. This man recommended bypassing the original roof and building from the peak a new structure thereby closing the opening and then roofing the new area. Securing the building and making it look better. We agreed on a price, and he went about solving that problem. It seemed it was one thing after another for a while. The aggravation would ease and then something would happen to cause consternation again, along with the monetary cost involved. Still drinking although not as much, I felt like I was being stretched to my limit. No ease to be had, I still was searching outside myself for something only I could give to me. My children were entering their teenage years and I felt incapable of the things I was charged with in life. Starting a new relationship with Noah, was not the answer, but I needed a distraction from all the turmoil my life was and with the background I had it seemed only natural to include a man in my existence. Eddie had invoked his teachings onto my son that I was morally unsound and the relationship with him was not good. When he came back from visiting his dad, he was not like a seventeen-year-old, rather he saw himself as a man and I was clueless as to how to help him. All these pressures were so profound because Emma was changing as well. My escape was into attempting to present stability and at the same time progress in my business.

I didn't ask Noah to move in with me, but he decided to because I came home from work one day and he had. We were close, at least that is what I thought, but the different cultures we were from quickly became obvious. He was black. Immediately he became critical of me. Being a business owner, it seemed he thought I had many more answers than I did. His criticism had to be tuned out because I could not deal with all it would entail to get him out of my house. Overwhelmed and drowning in all the pressures associated with being the head of all I oversaw, drinking became my only outlet. Knowing I needed to stop, I didn't know how, because it seemed every occurrence in my life I was being blamed for and punished with my closest ones turning against me as if I was causing it. Being from a large family, the choices I had made in my life had caused a rift with them. There was no one to identify with. My associates from work could not be my friends because their thoughts were I had everything. One girl stated as such one year when she drew my name at Christmas. Telling me she had gotten my name and said, "what do you get someone who has everything?" I sure didn't feel that way. Unable to know myself what I wanted, the basis for my existence was the two things this world is based on, money and sex. This is a truth that is a tough realization for us all. Finding any solace in them though is futile. What I wanted and needed was elusive. Haunted by my attempts to run away from the guilt of my first marriage, the physical abuse of my second and third marriage (I had married Warren twice), the drug abuse of my fourth marriage, here I was alone even though I was surrounded by people. Making money had lost its allure and the sexual urges that had gotten me in the relationship I was in were proving to be more of the same. Same problems, different faces. There is nothing to be said here other than I was not where I needed to be and was still searching for things only I could give myself. Noah was a hard worker, but his allegiance was with his family as it should be. He could not be other than. My affiliation with his culture was informative. Meeting his mother, sister and daughters, they were cordial and accepting of me. His father passed away the first year we were together, and he was devastated. Honoring his legacy was his main objective. Lack of understanding of his explanation of what his dad had tried to do for his family is more plain to me now than it could be then. He explained his dad had left each child with some property so they would at least have a place to live. Even though I had heard about racism, where I was from there were no people of color and I hadn't seen a black person until I started high school. My experience with the social hierarchy of our country was still not clear to me since I had been blessed with coming of age during the affirmative action period when I began my working career. I thought women had been granted equal rights, but it was only a pacifier put in their mouth to keep things being more of the same. I had heard the derogatory terms used regarding race and gender but only from the men in my life who had promised to love, honor and obey me and I them, as well as my father. Noah said he had never been outwardly cursed for his color excepting one time when he was in college. People in my life were accepting of us as a couple, the only blowback was from family members and rhetoric Dunk was spreading. Going as far as making malicious phone calls to me during the night saying all manner of vulgarities. I had moved on, and he was immersed in a takedown seemingly of me in any way it could be done, even though his brother and I were partners, he could control him and keep him where he wanted him. Not wanting to be in the battle I was in, it seemed it would not go away. It was a political smearing of me and my name to anyone that would listen, and many listened. Unused to such an onslaught, I reacted by ignoring it. Dunk in my eyes when we married was the smartest man I had ever known on an intimate level. For this reason and this reason alone, I succumbed to the notion of negating my own positive traits to be a tool in his tool belt of manipulation in ways detrimental to my personal well-being. Not recognizing the traits, it seemed everyone else in our circle accepted them, I resisted at my own peril. Learning a valuable lesson, one he was perfect at teaching, was not becoming engaged in a conflict when the opponent is on drugs, well versed in the art of manipulation, doesn't require sleep for days and allows their mind to accept all the ills of society as reality rather than corroboration with a mate to create the best possible solution. Again, not being heard reared its ugly head requiring the unfolding of a life I couldn't live.

My job entailed friendliness with patrons when I was out at other establishments. Noah and I would frequent other night spots up and down the road as a matter of habit to maintain friendly relations. Somehow his ego began to get the better of him. In my club, once we were together, we were accepted, but outside of the influence of this he began to show his dislike of my being friendly. Accepting a beer from one of my regular patrons even though the man sent us both one, his energy change could be felt. Approaching us to engage in conversation, Noah promptly drained his mug and said, "I'm ready to go". Since we were driving his car, maintaining a peaceful demeanor, I said I had to get home and followed him out the door. Never mentioning the incident again one way or the other. Experiencing this was grounds for expressing what had happened from my point of view but I did not. In my opinion, which is all I must work with, something such as this was common knowledge, yet this man did not know it and I was not going to explain something so elementary. This was an inkling we would not make it as a couple. My unwillingness to explain anything contrary to common sense was the beginning of the end. Knowing we could not continue; we did for three more years. Our end came when the pressure of my inexperience and tolerance of people acting as people will act when they are in the scene we were in, began to cause me to want the culmination of my efforts before it was time. Having three more years on my contract before my property was paid for, the situation I was in became unbearable for me. Even though Dunk and I were divorced, and I had gotten all I thought I wanted, I didn't really want it at all. It was making me sick. The perception others had of me was out of line with what I wanted for myself. Sometimes catastrophic events are blessings in disguise and turning things from what they are, to something better. Up to this point I was still dancing to a tune, not of my own making, rather operating on the next logical step in any environment we may find ourselves. There was no peace to be had working as I was with individuals looking to me to be the gear in making this machine roll, when the things being projected were not to my liking in any manner at all. I was in the wrong place, doing the wrong thing. Dunk and I had begun this enterprise and I looked to him as a wife will look to her husband, and I couldn't see or stand to be a leader of something I did not believe in. Not knowing I didn't believe in it though, I had to have a rude awakening to show me whatever it was I needed to learn. This awakening happened as awakenings will, all at once. Proving the phrase by Robert Burns, the best laid plans of mice and men often go awry.

May 1993, five thirty in the morning my phone rang. It was the alarm company; my building was on fire. Getting up, Noah and I drove down to the club, stood across the street at a convenience store and watched the building burn. It was a total loss. Shocked, I returned to my house after giving a statement to the police on the scene. It was arson they told me, but that was all they had. Not knowing what to think, there was much I had to do before considering my next move. Meeting with the insurance adjustor, I told him my thoughts on what I believed happened, but there was no proof of anything. All I really knew was my building was gone and it had to be cleaned up. Since it was so old there was asbestos siding under the siding we had put on, requiring special removal by an EPA certified cleanup personnel. Costing more than a regular cleanup, I contacted a company certified in said removal. Preceding the event of the fire I had made some drastic moves regarding employment in my business. Firing my partner as a stockholder and the three day a week barmaid that had been with me off and on since day one. I had met her while working at the club where I initially debuted, had become friends because we both had lived at the same apartment complex in the past, strange what will be a ground for friendship when we are in certain places in our lives. She had come to work at the first club we had opened, and throughout the years she would leave and always return after breakups of marriages, moves, and whatever changes she was making in her life, I was always there to offer a way to make a living. My club was the fairest, safest club for a woman to work because I was owner/ operator. Her allegiance to me, I felt was threatened by her allegiance to my partner. The stress I was under caused "a devil may care mentality" in me. Not giving myself credit for my tenure nor abilities, caused me to negate the importance of processing the gross experiences I had been through. I was ready to change everything about my life yet did not expect anything such as this. Of course, I felt it was my ex-husband after all that had happened. It might have been anyone though, because of the perspective people have of that type of business. Without first-hand knowledge they will usually assume the worst. The investigator told me arson is one of the hardest to prove crimes, the other one is murder, Google states burglary is number one, but this happened long before Google. Years later I met Dunk to say goodbye before I left the area, to move back home. He had gotten sick with liver cancer, and I took him to the social security office to file for disability. Asking him point blank if he had anything to do with the fire, he simply said no.

It took all summer of 1993 to tie up the loose ends of the business and get a buyer for the property as well as selling the liquor license. My partner, even though I had fired him, my attorney advised me to give him a portion of the proceeds from the sale. Meeting at the lawyer's office to complete the transfer of property and get the check, that part of my life was finally over.

Left with nothing to do I was at loose ends. Going from not having enough hours in the day to having too much time on my hands, being at home was somewhat torture. Turning down a myriad of opportunities coming my way, I didn't want to trust anyone with my allegiance and didn't want to go it alone. After what I had seen out of Noah, I knew he was not a viable partner nor mate for me, yet it took another year to come to the decision and garner the strength to end the relationship.

Part Four

Emma was in the last year of high school, and she had told me the year before she had joined the Navy. A recruiter had visited the school seeking recruits. I was okay with it. As life will goes, it seems everything happens all at once. Change has a mind of its own. Developing an attitude of acceptance was still in the making for me, though in its infancy. John F. Kennedy said, "change is the law of life. And those looking to the past or present are certain to miss the future". It seemed I was adrift in a sea without a compass. My whole reason for being was challenged and changing. I didn't know what to do with myself. Gary had moved into an apartment with a friend, Emma was leaving, I was in shock still attempting to find meaning in a seemingly meaningless world. Without focus, I was unable to think coherently. Applying for unemployment, I was receiving biweekly checks to keep me afloat, yet finding employment proved impossible. Deciding I must further my education, I began attending Community College. One of my first assignments was writing an essay of the most tragic event I had experienced. With my history it was a toss up to choose, yet the most recent was the loss of my business. In the past I had always found the stamina to continue in the face of adversity, but the calamity of realization of the hate others will harbor toward one another was overpowering. Noah felt I should be angry, but I could not feel anger nor hatred. Still unappreciative of the beauty of breathing and focusing on all the greatness of this life, I was numb. He became frustrated, unable to understand the magnitude of my mental state, trying in every way he knew to pull me out of it, his last resort was disdain toward my inability to do anything other than dwell on the injustice and wrongdoing that had come my way. So many realizations were hitting me at once. This was a classic example of kicking someone when they are down. Another truth coming to light, garnered now in hindsight but at the time incomprehensible. Through neither of our faults, it became clear to me we could not stay together. I could not give him the thing he needed, and he could not care for me the way I needed. Our life circumstance had changed so we had to change. The changes I was experiencing had to be navigated solo. Revealing to me that he had never lived on his own, he was scared to do it and at the same time looking forward to it. I wish I could say all these changes occurred smoothly and easily, however that was not the case. Realization comes all at once and once it came, I had to act. Recalling the exact instance when it hit me that we had to split up. I was sitting at the breakfast bar in my kitchen. He was at work. Journaling, I began the attempt to untangle all the issues between us, the things that were happening recently and in the past. All at once I wrote on the page, "you know what you have to do". That is when it hit me that I must make the break if I was going to continue the path of self-actualization required of ourselves in this life, we are blessed to possess. His criticism of me and my parenting tactics, business tactics, and all-around personage was at an end. Life had worn me "down to a nub". Psychological assault comes to mind as a description of the existence I had experienced as well as the nature of the male to dominate the female gender. My interpretation is based on my experiences. Bringing to light the idea of pairings of couples many times is a mismatch being adhered to because of a promise made of marriage vows taken. He had told me all women want is marriage. Having been married I did not want that, but he asked me to marry him because that was his belief. My attraction was physical and had I left it at that a whole lot of pain and hurt could have been avoided. Cultural conditioning, early life teachings and all false narratives can lead us as people astray causing us to live lives not of our creation, rather a mimicry of our parents' lives or some other authoritative figure we are in contact with. Hardship avoidance comes from an attempt to stay safe in a dangerous environment. The reason for our involvement was over and the gap that had emerged between us could not be traversed. Still, I had not told him we were through. Wanting to wait until Emma had left for the Navy because I wanted to keep things as even as possible until then. One evening I was attempting to eat, since I had lost so much weight, eating was difficult. He began with his tirade. Pushing my plate away, I looked at him and said, "it's over". Pushing my plate back in front of me, he became quiet and went to the bedroom to watch television. Finishing my meal, I took a walk, relieved I had told him, yet the finalization wasn't so easy.

Emma's graduation day came and my ability to navigate attending it was absent. Noah and I went. There were so many people there, I became overwhelmed and had to leave. Diving into my alcoholism, I began drinking as soon as we got back to my house. I don't know if I was having a nervous breakdown or what it would be called. All I knew was life had overtaken me and my functioning abilities were remiss. He, I believe, was thinking I was incapable of making any decisions and he would be able to take over my life and resources. All actions and behaviors pointed in that direction. Having borrowed money from me under the guise of making improvements to an apartment building he owned, when he took me to show me what had been done, the cost of improvement was not commensurate to the amount borrowed. Since I had gotten my insurance settlement both he and my bookkeeper had borrowed money from me. My bookkeeper had wanted five thousand dollars for a month only, to make improvements to his home to obtain an equity loan, and I lent it to him on a handshake, no interest, as a favor, since he had always given me a good price for his services. Noah on the other hand gave no repayment promise, in fact I think he was on a mission to take full advantage of anything he could. It seemed innate, the men in my life were acting as if I had no capabilities to manage all I had attained thus far. Having no words to express, nor desire to continue, my only option was removing him from my life. Having severed all ties with business associates, I was cleaning my life up. My children cannot be counted as associates because they are a constant, yet it began to seem they saw themselves as peers rather than deferring to me as their mother. Feeling invisible, diminished, estranged and at a loss for a reason to continue, my mind was all over the place.

Emma was scheduled to ship out for basic training in Orlando, Florida shortly after graduation, and from her disillusion of me she had left the house, and I didn't know where she was. Noah led me to think she and he were in touch, and I could not conceive where I was mentally. Everything was awry and made no sense. Needing time alone, not wanting to be alone, needing understanding, but having no person I could trust because all my relations seemed to be feeding on me. With nothing to refresh myself with other than drinking and marijuana, which wasn't working, my life was spiraling out of my ability to manage. The marijuana Noah got was laced with something I believe because I had never smoked anything having an effect such as it was having. Perhaps I am still searching to explain something that is unexplainable. When Emma left, Gary was having problems as well. Seemed the apartment situation with his coworker wasn't working out. Coming by my house one day, he said he needed to move. Probably they didn't pay the rent, but that was not his story. I told him he could come home, but he knew the rules of my house, and everyone had to work or be in school. Going into his room he collected some clothes he had left there and drove to Monroe County to his dad's place. Everyone was looking to me for strength and I was empty of anything to give. He had hated Noah from the start, even though Noah had initially tried to be a friend to him. He was twenty-one years old now and what society deems a man, even though becoming a man is much more than an age.

My world was falling apart. Nothing had ever hit me as hard as all I was experiencing. Having nowhere to turn, no person to share with, never once did I think of seeking medical help for the emotions I was having. Not knowing about rites of passage in life since it had never been a topic of conversation with anyone in my realm of acquaintance, I imagined I was losing my mind. Noah was all too willing to agree. It wasn't his fault because the culture he was from preached the same thing as the one I was from, and the one prevalent in our societal hierarchy. Bringing to my conclusion from my experiences that the structure is white man, black man, white woman, black woman with the children falling in behind. Without a cite of this as fact it is what my perspective caused me to conclude. He wasn't going to leave my house of his own accord. He felt it was a storm that needed to be ridden out. Both our behaviors deteriorated. Without going into specifics, I finally told him he had to leave on a certain day. Telling him I was visiting my family, I put all his belongings on my front porch, called him at work, told him my plan and that he was to come get them or else when I returned, I was calling salvation army to come get them. Having found out he was still married by going downtown and checking marriage and divorce records, I did not confront him with the knowledge of my discovery, because it only proved to me, he was not what he portrayed himself to be, rather an opportunist attempting to take advantage of the situation at hand. There was nothing needing proving to me. I saw the mentality of the person and the judgement passed on me was reminiscent of the same thing I had with Dunk. Finalizing the relationship still needed state interference because I still wasn't being heard. Taking for granted that I didn't mean what I was saying, I had to prove otherwise. Hard to do but a necessary step I felt I had to take to regain my equilibrium, I took an emergency protective order to cause him to listen.

Returning home from visiting my mother his things were gone from my porch, but we still had a court date to attend. It was so silly to me to have to go to court to make someone leave you alone. The judge felt the same way. Mentioning the money he had borrowed from me, I didn't ask for it back, the judge asked him if it was true, he had borrowed money. Not denying it, the judge told him he needed to make a repayment plan if he couldn't repay the amount all at once, which he could not do. Agreeing to a payment of 200 dollars a month until the debt was satisfied, which was a ten-month period. This person seemed to be under a spell of something other than the great person he truly, in his heart of hearts was. Sickened the stacking of society was revealing itself to me, I became unable to sleep, eat and otherwise practice healthy habits because the alcohol had me in its grasp. Emma was scheduled to ship out, and I didn't even know where she was. She had left home and was having no contact with me. Confiding in Cheryl, she said I had to go to the airport on the day she was leaving. She offered to go with me, even though I didn't want to go. Feeling as if she hated me and never wanted to see me again, when we entered, there was a page coming over the public address system, calling me to a certain gate. My heart came back to life for a moment. Approaching the seating area, I saw her sitting with several of her friends, and when it was time to board the plane, she never even acknowledged my presence. Brokenhearted, we left, taking Cheryl back to her home. I stopped on my way home to buy beer. Too many changes too fast to keep up with I was suffering emotionally, not knowing what or how to manage myself.

Dropping out of the program I was enrolled in, I decided I needed to take a certification course to ready me for employment upon completion, rather than a general curriculum. Not only this but I needed to train myself to a schedule because in my business I had the freedom to come and go without having to keep regular hours, and I was unsure I could. The curriculum at Vocational College offered a nine-month training course to teach how to work in a doctor's office. Nine months seemed an eternity to me, but I chose it because it was the shortest one offered, serving the purpose, I needed it to serve. My heart wasn't in it, even though I maintained a 4.0 GPA. Classes were Monday through Thursday, eight till eleven, then a break with my last class being one to three. I would go home, eat lunch, take a nap and return for the last class.

My plan was to stop smoking, drinking and maintain my health, but my addictions and neglect of self from the previous years had another plan in mind. Regression and boredom set in along with a lack of accountability is where I place the reason for what followed but it was more confusion and lack of perseverance along with an inability to count my blessings. My early life training of staying married and conforming to societal rules began to seem like it might be the way to go rather than making sensible decisions based on economics and feasibility. The people I was talking to at the time were incapable of assisting me with their word choice, they were pointing out my weaknesses more than my strong points as well as the progress I had made, colored by jealousy and wanting to dictate my next move.

My son and his girlfriend had moved in with me. His addiction to drugs was taking precedence in his life. They both worked but since my home was paid for, they paid nothing in rent nor groceries. It didn't matter to me about that, my concern was the chaos ensuing from his late nights and angry tirades. She was in love with him and attempted to convince him to stop but he was hell bent on pursuing the way of life he had chosen. Wanting to control my movements more than progress with his life, it seemed to me his disrespect was palpable. All of us needed therapy. After one angry outburst from him and their staying away for a couple days, I had decided they must leave. Stuffing their clothes into a couple of garbage bags, and cleaning the room they slept in, I went and lay down on my bed. My back was killing me, and my emotions were past the point of tears. Hearing a key in the front door, it was Gary coming in. He came into my room with a look of angry disgust on his face, threw my door key on the bed, said, "we're leaving". I replied, "your things are packed in your room", and he left after retrieving them. I never left my bed. Sick mentally I was glad they were gone because the upheaval was more than I could take. At the time I was seeing someone I had known from the club. This man had given Gary a job and tried to assist him but the pain he was carrying within outweighed any assistance anyone offered. Since the rules of my house could not be observed I felt I had no choice of any other action. Gary on the other hand was filled with conditioned blame for me because his dad had planted the seeds of blame in his fertile early mind. Drug addiction causes one to live in the past and words planted by authoritative figures in a child's life become the soundtrack of their inner thinking. Fault and blame are learned behaviors having no useful purpose in a progressive life other than a reference of what one doesn't want for oneself. At this point in time, I truly think my son hated me.

The person I was seeing at the time wanted to buy a club with me. Knowing this wasn't a good choice because of the health changes I needed to make, I broke up with him. He did not take it well. Once again trouble with the male species. Again, I had to take a protective order to cause myself to be heard. I had begun working Thursday through Saturday nights at a club to keep from using my savings. Graduation came in June 1995. Not attending the ceremony, I just got my certificate. Emma was home on leave at this time, but she was visiting her friends and besides I didn't want to attend the ceremony anyway.

Still working four days a week at the club, one evening as I was checking out a man came in, I had known for years by the name of Bronson Kingsley. He was drunk beyond driving so he had a man who had been a bartender at my club driving him around. Telling his driver to leave, he sat at the bar with his head down. After checking out he asked me if I would give him a ride to his house. This was the same man that had gotten in my car the evening my associate and I were celebrating my divorce years earlier. Unperturbed, I agreed to give him a ride. Maybe happenstance, providence or more likely because I was drinking myself, but there was no fear on my part of this person. Getting in my car, we drove the short distance to where he lived. Going inside we talked for a while and since I was drinking, I decided to stay the night. Explaining to him I was not interested in having a sexual rendezvous, he gave me the bed and he slept on the floor. He had been a frequent customer of the club for years and more of an admirer, rather than someone who saw himself as partner material.

Going home the next day, he accompanied me. Waiting while I showered and changed, we went to Tumbleweed restaurant for lunch and drank beer. We became a couple because I was so lonely and lost in my addictions to the point of thinking offering something solid to someone would elicit a positive response. It did not. Unable to solve my own emotional issues and ride the wave of self-recrimination to the other side, to be able to focus on my strengths, I engaged in a relationship with this man who was vested in the spirits evoked by ill treatment by his parents, along with alcoholism. He worked every day which was a trait he prided himself on, but the reliance of teamwork was remiss because of the experience of watching the relationship his parents had and his notion of what a man needed to be as well as a woman, caused an inability to trust himself and act out the things he had observed in his birth family, in our relationship. He was five years younger than me, and his emotional maturity was much more than that. Spending the next eight years of my life in a mess I well could have done without, but obviously needed because I could not move. Learning gratitude and appreciation of myself is the best takeaway of the experience. Emotionally abusive in ways I will not enumerate. The mess I had gotten myself into was incomprehensible, yet I learned valuable lessons of change creation. Before the actuality of the extent he would resort, in an attempt to dominate the situation, I sold my home and we moved to the farm he was buying which contained a two-room structure that had electricity but no indoor plumbing. Our goal was to build a house and make a home together, and things were going our way in many respects. The Water Company enacted an initiative to extend city water to parts of the County where it wasn't yet, so we were able to connect to it with only the cost of the water meter. Bronson could do anything as far as the building went and I could paint and assist him as needed. As a work team we were good together, as marriage partners the learned behavior of male dominance and hate would come out when he drank. His attempts at sobriety were futile. Having worked only a short time at a doctor's office after graduation from vocational school, quitting dancing in the club, I was unemployed and the realization of my mistake in selling my home became apparent to me and a rebuilding of self, had to take place. Recollecting this time, I was attempting to create a building of a life together to be honored and cherished, but it couldn't happen. Realizations are not easy to accept. It took two years for me to begin a job search and another year to gain employment. In the interim I had to leave the house many times when he drank to preserve what little self-respect I had left. Either getting a motel room or going to my sister's house. It was embarrassing to me to let anyone know the mess I had gotten into. Especially after the place I had been economically it was difficult for me to get my mind around the situation myself. Certainly not wanting my children to know I kept it from them as best I could.

Finally, after searching for employment, sending out resumes and getting no response, I was nearly convinced I couldn't find a job. Having to leave and go to Cheryl's house, she and I went to a fruit market near her home. Pulling into the parking lot, she said, "there's that place you've sent resumes to, you should go in there and see if they're hiring". "No", I replied. She continued to persuade me, assenting, after we left the market, I did just that.

Approaching the receptionist area, before I could ask for an application, there was a note taped to the top of the counter behind which she sat, stating accepting applications for quality assurance assistant. Telling her I wanted to apply for the position, she gave me an application to fill out. After filling it out she told me to wait a minute, the quality manager wanted to talk to me. Seating me in a conference room it wasn't long before a man entered, introduced himself and proceeded to interview me. Thinking my owner/manager position my club he mistakenly thought it was a restaurant. After explaining to him the nature of my business, he revealed he had been a county police officer earlier in his career and had made a run there. Not while it was my place but rather the person who had a club prior to my arrival on the scene. Leaving I was convinced I would not be hired. My confidence was at an all-time low after the things I had experienced with Bronson, thinking I could not make good decisions and was making backward decisions rather than forward ones. Returning to Cheryl's house, I told her I was going to the library to job search. When I got back, she met me at the door, telling me I needed to call the man I had interviewed with immediately. She said I had no sooner left than the phone had rung, and it was him, asking for me. I called and he offered me the position with a nice starting pay. Ecstatic, I was to start the following Monday. Calling Bronson that evening, I could hear the disappointment in his voice when I told him the news. Yes, I still was attempting to make my marriage work. Not wanting to get another divorce because the pattern was getting old for me. My starting pay was only a couple dollars shy of his pay and he had been at his employer for fifteen years. His jealousy was apparent. Staying with Cheryl the first couple weeks of working, once I got paid, I gave her some money and returned to my house. Bronson never wanted me to leave, and I didn't want to, it was as simple as the binding quality of addictions to cause the living of a life of misery perpetrated by a habit of behaviors. I had the same problem, and that was the cause of my being where I was. Continuing to work at this place for four years, until I was laid off in 2002, because of 9/11.

Bronson really tried to conquer his demon of alcohol. It became a once every three-month occurrence. Weird because it got to where I could know when it was going to happen the week before it happened. I don't know how this came to be, and I began to wonder if I was doing something to cause it. That is the profound effect the disease will manifest into, when parties blame another for actions that in no way can be attributed to them. Working together must take center stage for growth to occur. Once I was working it was harder to leave the house when he drank. More than once, I did leave the house. After telling him the imposition it was putting on me, one Friday I had a premonition he was going to come home drunk. Looking at the paper at lunchtime I saw an ad for an apartment nearby. Picking up my phone I called and set an appointment to meet the man at five o'clock that evening to look at it. Arriving at this decision had been a long arduous process, but once I made it, a load seemingly was lifted from me. Going to Cheryl's after work, I called Bronson when he got off work and told him my decision. Of course, he didn't want me to do it, but I had to change the scenario. I didn't want it either, it was my only recourse. The place was unfurnished, so I had to spend all day Saturday going to my house, retrieving some of my things. Garys girlfriend helped me pack my car with the essentials needed for the kitchen along with my clothes. Spending the evenings of the next week shopping for furniture, setting it up so it was livable, I settled in. The place had three rooms and a bath. Sufficient for me. Heated with a gas heater, and cooled with a window unit air conditioner, it was a converted pool house. Nice enough, the lady who owned it was retired, and maintained a residence in Monroe County. Her father lived in a house across the street, so he was the person to show me the place. Writing him a check for the rent and deposit I was uneasy, yet happy to not need to worry about having to leave home unexpectedly on short notice.

Still not owning the extent drinking played in the unfolding of events for myself, I continued to drink. Not as excessively as I had seen others do, yet the role it plays in our decision-making causes trouble for us, and anyone associated with us. Mainly our children, not only is this unique for me but it is the same for everyone. People who claim to be able to drink and it doesn't affect them, or their decisions are only fooling themselves. Having to experience the fallout of choices made while under the influence, best case scenario remorse, worst case scenario death. Either accidents caused by overindulgence or health issues caused by it. Unable to process my bad decision to get married again, sell my home, and now renting a small apartment, I would drink in the evenings. It wasn't long before loneliness set in. Not knowing what to do with myself, living alone in a new neighborhood, I gave in to the compulsion to phone Bronson one evening and we began talking by phone daily. Having signed a lease for a year, I still had three more months on it when I became sick with the flu. Coming home from work that day I was prepared to baby myself, watch television and go to bed early. It had begun to rain hard. Getting up from the couch, walking toward the kitchen I saw a rush of water coming across the floor from underneath the cabinets. The floors were ceramic tile throughout. Not knowing what to do, I picked up the phone and called the landlord. He answered the phone, telling me they were all sick over there. There was at least an inch of water standing in the living room and kitchen floors. The bedroom must have been on a higher elevation because it hadn't got in there yet. Taking my solid wood cherry tables into the bedroom my area rugs were sopping wet, and I told them as much. Saying I would take pictures of the mess for insurance, and they needed to do something tonight, he said they could not. Hanging up the phone, going into the bathroom to brush my teeth, I heard a knock on the door. It was the woman's husband, with a shop vac. He began sucking up the water. What had happened was the rain had come down so hard and fast and the ability to run off was insufficient, so it had nowhere to go except underneath the outside wall of the kitchen which sat flush with the driveway. When the alteration had been made from the pool house to an apartment the person didn't take into consideration the lack of runoff having anywhere to go. It was a flaw in construction and was covered with the driveway, so to correct it would entail digging up the driveway and creating elevation. I'm quite sure they were aware of the problem before renting the place, it was just a case of waiting for it to happen.

Realizing I must have residence access rather than depending on Bronson to manage his disease and I mine, I had begun the process of purchasing a house. Thinking Gary and his girlfriend could live there because the house payment was less than they were paying in rent. It was a better area as well, or at least I thought it was. Strange though how habits and attraction of like-minded people will find one another. This is what happened there.

The house was cheap, but needed total renovation, which I set about doing. Still in the apartment, I never put things back to rights after the flooding of the living room and kitchen. Spending all my spare time working at the house. Talking to HR at work, they allowed me to go four days a week, thereby giving me three days off to work on it. Bronson was a great assistant in the renovation, saving me a ton of money. HVAC, windows and cabinets were the only thing I had to hire done. We done the rest. Working on major projects on the weekend, and more minor things in the evening, we completed the remodel in three months. My landlady was not pleased when I broke the lease and wanted my deposit back. She denied the return of my deposit, so I composed a letter stating I would sue for damage to personal items resulting from the flooding, as well as the months

I had lived there while finding another place to live, plus my damage deposit. Getting the letter notarized and sending it certified mail so I would know she had received it, I moved back to the farm with Bronson. Since Gary was moving into the house, I decided to give my marriage another try. Telling Bronson, I would come back, but if I left again, I would not be back, he probably thought it was an idle threat because I had left and returned so many times. It was not. It was a promise I'd made to myself, and those promises cannot be broken. Having watched his parents' marriage play out the way it had, there was no other way for him to be other than the way he was. One evening after work I was at the house working. My cell phone rang. Answering, it was my landlady saying she was happy to forward me a check for my deposit and that after inspecting the apartment it was in better shape when I left than when I had rented it. She was gushing. Satisfied to resolve the issue, we ended the conversation in a friendly manner. Gary moved into the house in June 2001. He and his girlfriend were good tenants. Meanwhile Emma had gotten out of the Navy and moved into an extra bedroom at the house as well. Splitting the rent in half between her and Gary, she felt it needed to be a three-way split because Gary's girlfriend worked and lived there too. There was friction all the way around for me and I certainly did not need extra stress from an alcoholic husband, but it came anyway. At least I had a place to go rather than renting a motel room, yet I didn't want my children exposed to the ridiculous situation I had gotten into. Gary had a problem with alcohol and abuse issues, so it wasn't long before Emma moved out. Shortly after this Garys' girlfriend left him after eight years of being together, she found someone else. Not surprising to me, when he called me crying all I said was I was surprised she waited as long as she did, but love will cause us to put up with things we otherwise would not. Lack of family support and teaching will result in repetition of behavior in an attempt to right wrongs real or imagined. I hated the pain he was going through but there was nothing I could do. Up till this point they had always paid the rent on time, but after she left, he only paid one time and began drinking nonstop. This was in September 2001. Since winter was coming on, I could not put him out and he knew that. He had sublet a bedroom to a friend of his he had convinced to put the utilities into their name and was charging him rent to live there too. Until early spring this went on. Finally, when the weather began to warm up, I went by the house on my way to work. Unable to speak the words to him about what was going to happen, I had written it in a letter. Knocking on the door, I handed him the letter. Taking it he read it, tore it in half, threw it in the yard, looked at me and said, "you're my mother". Agreeing I said. "Yes, and you're my son". Turning, walking to my car, I went to work. It was a rough day for me. My letter to him stated the way eviction is to proceed. Thirty day written eviction notice, stating the reason for said eviction delivered in person. After this an order from the sheriff's office will be posted on the door giving them another thirty days after which they can be removed. There are special circumstances when it is family though as I found out when I went downtown thirty days later. If it is a family member it is on the person to solve the issue themselves. It was pouring rain the day I went downtown to the eviction office. My umbrella turned upside down as I rounded a corner and I got soaked, having taken a half day off work to do this, it was a miserable day. Going home when I got there Bronson was working, hanging drywall in the great room. When I told him about my day he said, "I would be crazy it that had happened to me". I said, "I am". It was a very difficult time. Bronson internalized the whole issue and began to allow his mind to wander. The following evening, he came home drunk, and I was unable to sleep. Barely getting through the remainder of the work week. Making a doctor's appointment, she gave me Tramadol which didn't help. Thank goodness, even though Bronson was drinking, he left me alone. Coming into the bedroom he said, "if he comes down that road, I'm blowing his head off". Looking at him I said, "go drink some more beer and leave me alone". Surprisingly he did. Going up to the house the next morning, which was Saturday, there was no answer when I knocked on the door. Jeppo, Garys pit bull was in the backyard, lunging at the fence. Using my key I entered the house. Everything was as if someone had just stepped out for a few minutes. Dishes in the sink, food in the refrigerator, furniture and all still there. Looking through the rooms the bedroom he had rented out was empty and smelled strongly of cigarette smoke and body odor. Bronson came up and changed the locks for me and the job of getting the place ready to rent began. Calling animal control they came to get the dog. Unsure of how long he had been left there, I feared him. The neighbors Gary was friends with came and said they had fed him a few times but had run out of the dog food Gary had left with them. There was a man at my job who had just bought a house and was looking for furniture, so I sold him the living room and bedroom furniture cheap. Some repair had to be made, but I was able to get it ready within a couple weeks after taking it back. Listing it with a property management company the utilities were transferred to them, and the sign went up.

They showed it a few times, but it was providence it didn't rent because one Sunday afternoon Bronson regressed to his habitual way of being, coming home drunk starting in with me. Premonition of the occurrence caused me to set the environment up to make a quick getaway. We didn't smoke in our house, we smoked in the garage, so when he got home, after making him something to eat, he sat at the table eating a sandwich. Finishing, he took the plate and smashed it onto the tabletop breaking it in half. Looking at me for a reaction, I gave none. Saying simply, "let's go out here and smoke", we went out and sat in chairs with a small table between us. He continued to drink. Remaining calm, I made small talk and directed the conversation as well I could to pleasant topics. Before he came home, I had placed an overnight bag in my car, staged my purse and keys on the hutch near the door leading into the garage, with my keys on top of my purse. He didn't notice any of these things. He said he had to go to the bathroom and as soon as he got up and went into the kitchen, I pressed the garage door opener, stepped inside the kitchen door, grabbed my keys and purse, got in the car, locked the door and waited for the garage door to open enough for my car to go through. Pulling out, he came out behind me, but it was too late, I was gone. Breathing a sigh of relief, to be free and have a place to go, I knew I would not return. Driving to my house, I lay on the floor in the kitchen attempting to sleep, but it was impossible because the smoke alarm batteries were going out and they were making the chirping noise they make when that is happening. Finding an old comforter I had used for a drop cloth when touching up the paint, I attempted to get some rest. When morning came, I went to McDonald's for coffee, waiting until I knew Bronson had left for work so I could go take a shower, and go to work myself, because he started earlier than I did. Piling enough clothing, towels and necessities to see me through the workweek, I drove to work. Putting in for the following Friday off so I could get myself set up to live in the house. Thankfully it was summer, and the weather was good. Sun always helps when going through less than stellar times.

Going to a furniture store, I purchased a box spring and mattress. That was all I had, but there was a refrigerator, microwave, washer and dryer so I figured I could make do until I could get the rest of my things from our house. Knowing divorce was imminent, my grief was more of the nature of disappointment in myself, rather than missing him as a person. We were talking during this time. He went to the store and brought my mattress and box springs to the house for me. He wasn't displaying any behavior that was dangerous when he wasn't drinking. The dynamics between us was cordial.

Returning to work the following Monday, there were no inspectors in the office. My manager came in shortly after my arrival. Informing me there had been a layoff the previous Friday and I no longer had a job. Weird as it may sound, I was relieved. Needing the time to reconcile myself to the situation at hand. When I arrived home, I took a nap.

There was no cancellation fee from the property management company for cancelling the contract. Just a matter of phone calls to utility companies to switch service into my name and tell property management I had changed my mind. Relaxing after so many years of upheaval, felt good. Applying for unemployment benefits, once more I could breathe for a spell.

I had not heard from Gary since I had put him out of the house in early spring. Here it was July, with his birthday coming up and I was missing him terribly. I had been trying to locate him to no avail. I got him a birthday gift and kept it for a while before taking it back to the store for a refund. Emma was working on a shift running from eleven o'clock at night till three in the morning. She would visit me in the afternoons. It was good except for the sadness of missing Gary. Still, I had not filed for divorce because I wanted to work things out with Bronson to reach a mutual agreement, thereby saving us both money and expediting the process. No such luck.

I searched the want ads for jobs, sent resumes, filled out applications at numerous places but to no avail, as well as looking for furniture for sale. Finding a living room set, dining room set and an occasional chair for three hundred dollars, I called and set up a time to come look at it. Since I had no way to get it Bronson brought his truck and we went to get it. I bought it all. Spending my time working on my house and pursuing a job, I was quite content. It was July 22, 2002, when I left the farm.

Sitting at the table on an evening, in early October after living there about three months, there was a knock at my door. Unperturbed, I answered and there stood my son with a bucket of wings from Buffalo Wild Wings and a six pack of Budweiser. Ecstatic to see him I allowed him in. He had been staying with a man he worked for just a few streets from my home. There was no bed for him to sleep in, so he slept on the sofa the first night he was there. Thinking we could cohabitate; my idea was to level the playing field of the obstacles holding him back. He needed to get his driver's license and secure a vehicle, all of which I was willing to help him do. Beginning immediately to do these things he seemed cooperative to a degree, yet he wanted to drink every day and couldn't focus on anything else. Working with him we got his license, but it was an all-day endeavor. Forgetting the things he needed to take with him we drove to where the testing took place, only to have to return to the house to retrieve what he had forgotten. We had the documents ready to go, yet it seemed he didn't really want to do it. After doing this we began looking for a used vehicle for him to buy. Seeing a red Toyota pickup at a used car lot, we stopped, and he test drove it. It was low miles and he liked it. Coming back the next day, after talking about it we made the purchase. I was a co-signer for him. Next in order was insurance. Contacting several companies, it was astronomical the amount of money wanted to insure him. Finally calling my agent at State Farm, I was able to add him on mine with just a little upcharge. Doing all these things, he was ready to go. The payment on the truck was weekly. Reminding him when he got paid, he would yell at me saying things like, "get off my back" and other rude things I didn't understand. The insurance I simply paid. He began not coming home until late at night, staggering drunk, and all the behavior associated with it. The air mattress he slept on had a leak in it and would go flat each night. He made good money but didn't seem concerned with using it to create a better existence for himself. I didn't know what to do. Unable to talk to him about anything without being yelled at, I had to get a job to maintain my sanity. This is not the way I wanted to live.

Early December 2002, Gary was late coming home, so I took the phone into the bathroom with me to soak in the tub. Scared I'd miss a call in case something happened, and sure enough the call came from jail. He'd gotten locked up for drunk driving. He had rear ended a woman exiting the freeway causing injury to her and damage to both vehicles. All this was making me crazy. Telling him I would not come get him, the best take away for me was at least I knew he was safe for the night. Consequently, the truck was towed to a shop for repair, then repossessed. At the time I never considered the liability I had as far as my insurance was concerned.

Answering an ad for a driver for a pharmacy company, in the east end of town, located thirty minutes from where I lived, the man who interviewed me did not think I was right for the job. Even though it was much less than what I had been making per hour, I felt getting employment was paramount for my survival mentally. Later the same company had an ad for a Pharmacy Tech listed, so I applied for that position. The same man interviewed me. Hiring me he joked, he had to hire me because I kept coming for interviews. Beginning in January 2003, the job was brutal for me. Not used to standing on my feet all day, and having improper shoes, I had never gotten so tired nor had my feet hurt so much as they did that first day. Since my shift didn't begin until nine in the morning, the evening after the first day, Gary and I went to Value City and I bought a pair of K Swiss shoes to wear the next day, it was a big improvement.

Gary was under house arrest after getting out of jail. Refusing to talk about it with him, I let him deal with it because my emotions were shot. He got a lawyer and didn't lose his license even though I don't know how that was managed. He worked and gave all his money to the lawyer. After the truck was fixed, it was repossessed. Back to square one. Continuing to work at the pharmacy, the weather turned bad one day while I was at work. Snowing, sleeting alternately, and I got a call on my cell phone.

It was the receptionist at State Farm Insurance where I had been insured for the past twenty odd years. She told me my insurance was cancelled at midnight that night. This was on a late day for me, meaning one week I went in at seven in the morning and got off at five in the afternoon, the next week I went in at nine and stayed until closing. If there was a late admittance to a nursing home we served, we stayed until we got the prescriptions the person needed filled. Frantic, I didn't know what to do. Telling my supervisor the situation, I left work and drove to an Allstate Insurance office. Walking in I was in tears. The agent saw my distress, got up, came to me, put his arms around me and we prayed together. I'll never forget that. Such a small gesture but it meant so much to me at the time. Purchasing auto insurance, I returned to work. That evening driving home, the freeway was covered with snow. Unable to see the lines separating the lanes, I followed the taillights of the vehicle ahead of me until it exited, after which there were no other cars on the road. Driving at a slow speed I finally arrived home to my son sitting on the sofa with his ankle monitor on. His probation officer had been there earlier that evening to check the monitor, and there were footprints on the light-colored carpet in the living room, where he had walked across the yard getting his feet muddy, rather than using the sidewalk. What a way to end my day.

My windshield wipers began not clearing the windshield and having them changed didn't help with the problem. The arm of the wiper seemed to be bent. How something like this could happen was beyond me, and I couldn't find anyone to fix it. After driving home in the mess of the snowstorm and realizing there was a problem with them, I had to get them fixed. My car was low mileage, but it was having a problem as well. Taking it to an auto repair shop for repairs, I spent an entire Saturday, an off day, spending over four hundred dollars, only to leave and still had the same problem. Life was becoming overwhelming. After leaving the shop, I made an impulse decision to stop at a dealership on my way home. Making a left-hand turn into the dealership, yes, the same dealership I had been propositioned for prostitution at, years ago. It had been closed and reopened, so it was all new people working there. I had seen a Chrysler PT cruiser and liked it, so I test drove one they had on the lot. Wanting a red one, the salesperson told me he would find a red one for me and call when he found it. Leaving, I stopped at a Chevrolet Honda dealership where Noah used to work. Met at the door by a young man eager to sell me a car. Test driving a new Chevy Chevelle I think it was, it didn't have a sturdy feel about it. Espying a 2002 Honda Accord, red in color I asked to look at it. Retrieving the keys, as soon as I sat in the driver's seat, I knew I had to have it. The feel was sturdy and sure. I had not had that feeling for ages. Beginning the process of the purchase I spent the next several hours making the car mine, driving it home that day. It was the best decision I had made in a long time. When I got home, I cleaned the whole house. It was strange that I got a phone call that evening from the sister that had assisted in my birth. She had never called me before ever, but we chatted for an hour. Telling her I had just bought myself a car that day she said good for you.

My bank at the time was having a sale on loans. The requirements were it had to be at least five thousand dollars over the amount borrowed. Combining my house and car payment and taking the five thousand and putting it in my checking account, I was able to satisfy my car loan and the combined loan amount was manageable on the small amount of money I was earning. It was a good move because I went from a thirty-year loan to a fifteen-year loan and reduced my payment significantly. My issues were not financial, they were personal. The people I was surrounded by seemed unable to manage themselves and expected me to manage their affairs for them. My expectations of the things feasible for them to do were not happening, thus causing me grief mentally, physically, emotionally and financially.

Bronson was still in my life because he was the only one who could remotely assist me, yet even though he was a mechanic by trade, he refused to look at my windshield wipers when they were acting up. My confusion was great, yet it seemed the car and the refinance combination loan caused a breakthrough of sorts for me. I began to think maybe I could make some good decisions.

Super bowl Sunday fell on January 26, 2003. The next morning while getting ready for work, the phone rang, it was Cheryl calling with some news I was not prepared to hear. She told me her oldest son had gone to a Super Bowl party at a friend's house and Bronson was there with a date. A young girl of seventeen years old. He had taken a new truck the previous Friday to test drive. They had allowed him to keep it for the weekend. Of course, he was drinking and letting this young girl drive him around in the truck. Feeling as if I'd been kicked in the stomach by a mule, I gathered myself and went on to work. It was an early day for me, so I was home by five thirty. Needing someone to follow him to the dealership to give him a ride back home after dropping off the truck, he came by my house to see if I was able to do it. Not telling him I knew what I knew I began asking him questions about the day before. He was visibly nervous when I began talking about the Super Bowl and parties I had had in the past at the club. He finally became so agitated that he just got up and left. Asking him later how he got home from dropping off the truck, he said he had ridden the bus.

Calling an attorney, getting an appointment the following Wednesday, which was an off day, I filed for divorce. The cost was fifteen hundred dollars retaining fee, so it had really increased in price from previous filings. The lawyer smelled money, that was the reason for the charge. Wanting to get it over with was all I wanted, but it was not to be the case once again. It's not that I take my marriage vows lightly, I do not, but I am short on forgiveness of the liability associated with underage drinking, the possibility of an accident and the possible fallout in the event something happened. Being still attached to him legally by marriage was cause for consternation. None of what I had going on in my life at the time was what I wanted to experience and there seemed to be no way to escape it.

Gary had moved in with a bartender who worked at a bar he frequented. Emma had moved out of her apartment, back in with me and I continued to work as a pharmacy tech. As always for me, drinking was a culprit causing, as it will, bad decisions and ill-conceived ways of living. Yet it seemed my only escape was drinking. Needing, rather wanting a connection to someone, I began frequenting the bar where Garys girlfriend worked. This period of my life is confusing and hazy. Learning more about human nature than I would like to know. Predatory practices and angles to drag a person down through pretending to like them, but looking for a safe harbor from life's storms, I met a man who was doing exactly that. He had no clue about who I was as far as personal uniqueness, which is the thing needed to build a relationship on. Presenting as a family man, once I got to know him and the people, he called his family, it was obvious to me he was being tolerated rather than admired by these people. Having married a woman many years ago who had nine children was his claim to greatness. His career had been that of a bartender, so he thought he knew people and presented as such. After meeting for drinks a few times, he invited me to where he lived for dinner after work one evening. Meeting his daughter who was a stepdaughter, he called his daughter. She was the same age as me. Unhealthy from birth, she was a smoker and had COPD. He informed me later that she was in love with him. The other family members allowed him to live there because otherwise this woman would be alone, and she needed someone there with her. Working downtown Little Rock, sometimes she rode the bus so he could use the car. Drawing social security, he spent his days at the bar until his money ran out, then he would hit her up for more. Cleaving to me, his thoughts were along the lines of moving in with me, and he said as such. Unloading him proved to be an unfavorable task but it had to be done. It had gotten in a short period of time to the point where he would ask me to pay for our drinks, get mad when I worked overtime, and all manner of ridiculous behavior. Without calling him out on it I simply stopped answering the phone when he called and quit going places where he was. It still caused tumult in my life because I was vulnerable before I knew the terms true meaning. It was causing me to do things I would not normally do. Lonely, making barely enough money to live on, I wanted a connection but not at the price this person expected me to pay. He was becoming a nuisance. A determining factor was when he asked me to go to the gambling boat, then on the way there saying we needed to go to the bank and get money. Getting in the car, I was driving, I asked him which bank he needed to go to, and he said yours. That's what I mean by ridiculous behavior. It was a distraction to make my time go by in the interim of my divorce, and that's about all that can be said for it.

Gary was in and out of my house and Emma had met a young man who would become her second husband. With them both young adults, him being thirty years old and she twenty-six, I still felt responsible toward them, and the load was extremely heavy because when they are small their movements can be controlled but once they are this age it is not the case. Causing me to feel emotions I didn't know how to feel. Other people were involved too. Garys girlfriend had four boys. Where did I fit into that equation? I did not know. Lost is the best description I can conjure of this time. My saving grace was the awful, low paying job I had, but I was grateful for it because it was the only place I felt as if I was being productive in any way. Other areas of my existence were nearly intolerable. Imperceptible to onlookers, I was the only one who knew the inner turmoil I was dealing with.

Painfully lonely, disillusioned with life, stuck in mire it seemed I was incapable of getting out of, I was looking for love and acceptance in all the wrong places. Rather than inside, I was still seeking validation from outside sources. Grocery shopping at Meijers on an off day, while at the checkout, a man behind me in line struck up a conversation with me by saying, "do you need some help drinking that beer?" "No", I replied and continued with the checkout. Before I could get out the door, he accosted me and continued talking. His left eye was cloudy and had something wrong with it. Asking what happened he proceeded to tell me he had been cutting a tree down for someone without wearing safety glasses. Some sawdust had gotten in his eye, and he thought nothing of it at the time. Next morning his eye was aching and sore. Going to see a doctor, they informed him he had a fungus infection in it like the fungus that grows on tomato plants. Treating had proven fruitless, for several reasons. The medicine he was treating it with was not used properly, I found this out later when we became a couple. He retired from the electric company by taking an offered buyout. This man was personable and talented but as with so many of us humans he was an alcoholic and occasionally used harder drugs. Being a good, kind natured soul was his salvation. Religious and God fearing when he done something he felt was wrong he would worry about himself and try to do better, but, as with many of us, he would regress habitually.

With my son moving in and out, the inability to find any place in my home where it felt like I fit as a person, I listed my house for sale. Wanting to ask ninety thousand dollars, the agent I worked with talked me into reducing the price to eighty-nine nine. She thought it sounded better. Agreeing, the sign was erected. There were no good memories there for me. Nothing but ill treatment of myself by myself and others who didn't know any better. Walking out that door, I went to a bar on the way to my boyfriends' house. That is what I called him, even though the relationship was never much more than a warm body to be around. His addictions caused him to be uninterested in sexual relationships as well as his religious beliefs of thinking people should be married before copulating. Not that we never had sex, we did, but it was not a big part of our life. Our drinking and his depression were the basis for our relationship.

There was no movement on the selling of my house. The agent would call me weekly and tell me she didn't know what was going on because there weren't even any lookers. Outside reasons was my reason for listing it in the first place. Getting awakened in the early morning hours when I had to work the next day by voices yelling in the front of my house, looking out the window, I saw a car with the passenger door open, dome light on, a man standing beside it cursing and screaming at the female driver. Recognizing the man as my son and the woman as his girlfriend, without turning on a light, I went out the back door, stood at the gate at the end of the driveway, and smoked a cigarette. Never venturing to the front of the house so they could see me, after a few minutes they were gone. Deciding right then and there it was over for me with his unmanly behavior, the next day I called the agent I had worked with on the purchase of the house four years earlier. This was a rash decision but it was irrational behavior I was dealing with so that is my reasoning at the time. My thoughts were if I could not manage what was happening at my home, I was undeserving of a home. After I left the house everyone else did as well. Emma moved in with her boyfriend, and the next I heard of Gary he had moved in with another girl he had met at the bar.

The listing with the agent was for 120 days, with no action I had decided and was hoping it didn't sell, because I needed to live there, but couldn't stay there with all that was going on. Since it was empty, I wanted to go back and attempt to heal the trauma I was suffering, yet one week before time was up, a man from Georgia that had recently retired looked at it and wanted it at full asking price. The closing took place at an attorney's office. Since my divorce wasn't final Bronson had to be there to sign allowing me to sell it. We were together when I bought it. This seemed insane to me because it was my money from a mutual fund I had before we were married, I used for the down payment, and it was me who made the payments, but that's the law.

I didn't have anywhere to put my furniture, so I asked for time to be able to make some plans for myself. Contacted by my agent, she said the man wanted to buy everything that was there, which would have been great, but later changed his mind so I had to make some quick adjustments. Having seventeen days to empty the house, I rented a room at my boyfriends' house, took my bed, packed all my kitchen things as well as pictures from the wall etc., storing them in an extra bedroom at his home. Paying him 250 dollars a month to stay there until I could make other plans. His place was a mess. It was impossible to do anything about it because he was a hoarder. The type of hoarder they portray on the television show Hoarders. Since his retirement, he didn't know what to do with himself other than drink, worry about the mess, get past his hangover and do it again. This was an in between time for me and I knew it. He didn't know where or who he was, and if a person doesn't realize where they are, there is nothing they can do about it. Depending on someone else to solve the problem for them, they are contrary to any suggestions made and argumentive to the point of ignorance.

Nearing the end of the seventeen days, Cheryl, knowing of my situation, had been visiting family in the country, called me and said she had sold my furniture to our nephew. She and her man would meet me at the house, pick it up and deliver it to him. Such a life saver for me at the time since she did just that, delivering me a check for it. Once more I breathed a sigh of relief only to delve deeper into attempting to solve the problems of misery I was living. Brings to mind the saying, "pain is inevitable, misery is optional". Misery was my companion during this time out from life. It was a time out that I knew would end, I just didn't know how, or when. Each day or evening (depending on the shift I was working) when I got off work, I frequented a bar nearby where I was staying and drank beer until it was time to go to bed. Sometimes my boyfriend accompanied me, most times I went alone. Since it was only a couple blocks away, I didn't worry about getting locked up for drunk driving. It could have happened, but only by happenstance. Whatever will be will be was my attitude at the time.

Living a life unlike anything wanted for oneself requires a breaking down of self to the point of near degradation, or such was the case for me. Downcast, unsure and captive within, I was not able to find reasons for going on, yet I somehow knew this road must be traveled because here I was, and I was on it. It was better than being married, and dominated by someone fostering their hatred onto me, because I was free to choose even though I was free falling for around six months. Work was becoming more intolerable, especially when we were told we were to work harder and get no raise in our pay. Knowing the role I played there, the supervisor sought to denigrate and demoralize rather than uplift and energize. I don't know whether this was a style of leadership he was conscious of, or if it was his natural personality. It was the energy he exuded to me. Our rate of accuracy was 99.9 percent, yet when I made a mistake with a prescription, by filling it with Calcium D rather than Calcium he called me out on it in a harsh manner in front of everyone, saying "you are going to kill someone with mistakes like that." Perhaps he was having a personal issue having nothing to do with the workplace which can happen to anyone, and I understood that, yet when he apologized to me, he took me into a room with just the two of us to do it. Respect was lost on my part, deciding then and there I would compose a letter of resignation. Turning it in the next day to HR, I gave two weeks' notice and nothing was acknowledged about my leaving until two days before the last day I was to work. Coming to stand beside me while I was filling prescriptions, he asked about my letter, saying he had found out about it only that day. Telling him I had submitted it two weeks ago he said no one had made him aware. The lead tech asked me about it at a break we were taking at the same time. She didn't want me to leave because I made her job easier by my attitude and ability to assist others in getting along. She told me if it was more money, I wanted she would see that I got a raise. My reasons were deeper than money. my whole existence needed a makeover and money had nothing to do with it. Trauma from my retirement being swept away from me when my business burned, the realization that my son at thirty years old had dedicated himself to drug use, the failure of my marriages, the homelessness I was experiencing was part of the reasons, more so than money. My fall from grace was devastating along with further realization of the hierarchy we inhabit as humans was becoming more and more a reality. Seemed there was no reason for my existence anymore since things had manifested as they had. Dwelling on and practicing the negatives of life, my will to continue continued, albeit in a confused and scattered state. Moreover, my mother was not doing well, and the futility of life was sinking in thinking about all she had experienced to wind up with even more suffering. Visiting her at my sister Susan's house where she lived, Susan had quit her job to take care of her. Removing her from the nursing home where she surely would have died, sooner than she did. Sitting at the table perusing the want ads I saw an ad for factory workers with a starting pay of 12 dollars an hour that was being built there in my hometown where my sister lived. This was a deciding factor in my decision to seek housing and employment there. Deciding to do something and then doing it is a process, and not without setbacks. Setbacks are a way of life, yet with the life experience I had along with the knowledge I had, I was at the point, with a "nothing from nothing leaves nothing" attitude and I made the decision to pursue it. Taking this literally, it became a mantra of mine irrespective of everything and anything. It truly was a freeing place to be. Returning to the room I was renting, thinking of my decision choices, I began weekly or at least biweekly visits to see my mother. Taking a walk around the neighborhood where Sue lived, with Cheryl who was there to assist with moms' care, I saw a for sale sign in a yard for a cute little house. Going up and knocking on the door I asked to look at it. Inviting us in the man allowed us to look around. It had four rooms and a bath with a basement. Telling him I would go to the bank and make my money available to purchase it, I proceeded to do it that very day. Once I made the arrangements the couple began to hedge on selling. We had agreed though that I would buy it, but he upped the price five hundred dollars over the initial purchase price, he said because of the dishwasher. Saying it was new and he had forgotten about it when telling me the asking price. Not wanting to lose out on the house because I loved it, it was affordable and had been totally renovated, I could see myself living there, I agreed to pay the initial price, plus the addition to it. Angered, Cheryl wanted to argue about it, but I told her it was okay. Having been looking at places in Little Rock that were not livable at twice the cost, I knew this was my best bet on having a place to "hang my hat". The man said the day I knocked on the door was the last day they were going to leave the sign up. This is why I gathered he was the one wanting to sell and the wife was not. She was pregnant and they had a four-year-old, who sat on the steps as I walked out, visibly upset I had bought the house.

Going back to retrieve my things from where I had been staying, check my P.O. box, put in a change of address and tie up loose ends, I got a phone call from Dunk. He was sick and had applied for disability. Needing a ride to the Social Security office, I agreed to pick him up at a Waffle House. When he walked out the door of the restaurant, I didn't recognize him. He was haggard looking. I hadn't seen him in years, even though we had been talking by phone occasionally. Harboring no ill will toward him, I felt more pity than anything. Choices and decisions dictate all our life's destiny and he had made some dire ones. I had never seen anyone in my life as intelligent as the man, yet the psychological aspect of our relationship was such there was no way it could survive. Dependence, attachment, viciousness, fault, blame and excuse making; too many negatives to mention were at play. Manipulation of my positive attributes by him caused me to know, in hindsight there was no way we could survive as a couple, even though our breakup was one of the hardest things I ever went through I learned much about myself. During our drive we conversed about trivial matters initially, but his mind was wandering and reflected in his words. When I told him my plans to move back home, it was obvious that he was chagrined by my decision. Somehow it surprised me he would feel that way after all the years that had passed. He said he wished we had sold out and moved there while we were still married. We could have opened a restaurant. We could have done good; we could have made it anywhere together. It was sad to see the man he had been, reduced to what he had become. Even then I did not fully realize the fatalness of the disease he had, telling him he was going to beat the cancer eating away at his liver, he knew he could not. That was a sad day for me.

Part Five ————————

The closing date for my home was set for May 8, 2005. Meeting at the bank we made the change, but they still wanted more time to evacuate because they had no place to move. Giving them more time, they finally moved in with the woman's mother, so I was able to get what I had left together, gaining possession. An excerpt from my journal depicts my mindset on the first night there, May 23, 2005, was the date because of the wait on moving in, as follows: "I am spending the first night in my new home. It is a very old house, but new for me. I feel at peace here. The only ones who have been here have been my family. I have around me what things I have left. Familiar things, comforting things, my things. I have been displaced for a long time. I miss nothing nor no one. There is much I need, but I will get all I need. Heavenly Father bless this my home and keep me safe from all wrongs. Open my mind to all I can be and give me the words of expression as needed. Help me find my place. Give me back my mind and keep me safe Amen".

Strange how early childhood teachings will manifest into our existence and thoughts when we are creating change for ourselves, causing a regression along with a throwback to teachings whether they are beneficial or not. Maybe this isn't true for everyone, but it was for me at the time. Fear will rear its ugly head, having no person to confide in because of false labeling and comparisons that

160

had been made of me by immediate family members, I experienced a regression of mindset, taking me down a familiar yet undesirable road. Small town, small minds. Labeling is prevalent and there are gender related expectations assigned to people. Thinking outside the box is discouraged in my family and since I was attempting to acclimatize and integrate myself back into the society, I had been absent from, I can more easily see why I succumbed to what unfolded next.

Catty corner across the street from my house there was a rental house. Late at night there would be loud music coming from the place and all the lights would be on. Of course it attracted attention. Directly to my left there was an elderly lady living alone. She was friendly to me and was a widow. Since I smoked, but didn't do it inside the house, sitting on the front porch on a Sunday morning the person living in the catty-corner house was leaving and pulled to the side of the street to tell me they were going to McDonalds for breakfast, could they get me something? Saying no I was fine, I really needed to leave it there, but I did not. I love McDonalds pancakes and sausage, so I quickly changed my mind and decided to get them. Returning with the food, I invited him in, we ate at the makeshift table, which was a metal patio table I had found in the basement, that I had put a spread on. From his looks it was apparent he was a heavy drinker. Bloodshot eyes, red nose, flushed complexion and shaky hands was a dead giveaway. Familiar looks to me from my background. Finishing our meal he took leave. It began to be customary that he would venture over when I would be on the porch smoking. My elderly friend, the widow noticed and, in her way, attempted to caution me about getting too close with a drunk. Once more though my vices caused me to enter an arena, I would have been better to have avoided. Making the aforementioned statement is a judgement though that would take away from my life story and even though it unfolded the way it did is the way it needed to go for me to remain safe. I honestly believe things transpire in our favor when we have good intentions for all, no matter what detours we experience. It's the only way to learn what we need to know.

He invited me over to listen to music, and of course drink some beer. I accepted the invitation. Once we began drinking, we didn't stop until daylight. I awoke in his bed. Feeling ashamed, I got up, walked across the street to my house, took a long shower and tried to get over what had happened. He was still asleep when I left. Difficult as it is to recall, I must own the part I played. Again, it was vices that led me into the involvement even though I knew it was not the best thing for me. Wanting to change my habits and create an existence I could be healthy in was my desire, yet this person had different ideas and being raised as I had been to defer to the male species, I succumbed to the suggestion that we could reside together as a couple. My financial situation was intact and well planned as far as having enough money set aside for six months' leeway before I had to begin dipping into my savings to subsist, so there was no problem there. I had already gotten a job as a waitress at a diner there in town. Even though I didn't make a lot in tips, I was able to pay my expenses, so there was nothing to blame it on other than the drinking. Drinking was our only commonality, and I was on a pathway to sobriety and this person was not. Discussions about cohabitation were only talked about when we were drinking and that was all the time, when we were together. My house was much nicer than where he lived. He saw himself living there.

Thinking I needed medical insurance, I continually was looking for employment offering it. MacDonalds offered a form of health insurance, so I accepted the position of assistant manager at the store in the neighboring town. It was day shift for the training, so I was able to remove myself from drinking for a while. Beginning work there was not a good fit for me. Not wanting to offend, and allowing someone to take over one's life is detrimental to any personal perceived progress. I didn't want to hurt anyone's feelings so I, because of adverse training in the way I was brought up allowed my own space to be invaded by a person with an adverse mentality and equal disrespect for women. Convincing me it would be good for us to live together, I allowed this to happen. Coming home from work one day he was moving in. He retired from the military and worked dispatch for the county sheriff's office. Working, he said to try to control his drinking. He was an abuser and saw me as an easy target. This turned into more of the same thing I was attempting to get away from. Once he was in my house, I began thinking about how I could get him out. Crazy sounding but how else can crazy behavior sound? I wasn't looking for someone to blame, this person was. It's all so many people know, are raised with and thus perpetuate.

The job I had in mind when I moved to this part of the country, for some reason, was not calling me to come to work there. Not accepting this I, after applying for employment on more than on one occasion, called the H.R. person and was sent to voicemail. Leaving a message to the effect that I had relocated, bought a house, had a car and was a reliable person wanting to work at their company and could not understand why I wasn't being called to work. Needing this to go my way I had gotten to the point where I could not hedge any longer. Thinking this would either work, or rule me out entirely, I was somewhat surprised when later that same evening she called to set up an interview time for me with the hiring manager. Happy to finally have something go my way, I thought maybe I could change my existence after all. I was hired and began working there. Even though this person was still in my house I had to rule out all thoughts about it and concentrate on working and rest. Since I had stopped drinking except for a beer when I got off work, he would still be up because we both worked second shift, he began drinking more it seemed. He had begun talking to a woman from North Carolina in a chat room, expecting me to be jealous and when I wasn't it angered him. Everything about this situation was foreign to me but seemed commonplace to him. Ignoring him, I just went on with my existence. He stayed up all night and I never knew when he slept, ate or anything about his activities. She started calling me on the phone trying to argue with me. Again, crazy making behavior. Trying to choose a time when he wasn't drinking to tell him to leave was the focus of my thoughts. It was not easy to do. Finally, one day before I was going out the door, headed to work I simply said, "I want you to move, as soon as possible". Leaving, without giving any time for a reply, I was relieved to finally have spoken the words.

Returning home that evening, he was gone. Next day he called and asked me to go with him to look at a place he had rented to move into. Agreeing, he came over. He had spent the night at his mother's house. Driving to the place, it was a mobile home. Trashed out, it was a mess. There was no heating unit nor air conditioner, it was unlivable. Having already paid a deposit and rent for a month, I told him there was no way anyone could live there. Deciding to stop payment on his check he had written, he said he needed me to assist in finding him a place. My sister, Roberta had some mobile homes she rented out. Contacting her to ask if she had anything available, she did. It wasn't completely empty, but she allowed him to move in. Not all, but many of his things were still at my house. I was just glad to have him secure something away from me. The place had central heating and air as well as being fully furnished.

It was peaceful having him away from my place. My son had been living with a girl and they weren't getting along so it was somewhat of a blessing for me when he showed up at my house to stay a few days. It kept me from being alone, because this person I was removing had proven to be mentally unstable so by Gary being there it was a deterrent. The place I worked at made air bags for the automotive industry, so when they shut down for two weeks in the summer we did as well. Perfect timing for me to complete the removal of this person from my home. Refusing to get the remainder of his things from my house, using Gary's truck he and I loaded everything up and took it to the trailer he was renting. He refused to answer the door, so we piled it under the tree in the front of the trailer. Gary felt bad about it, but I didn't. This person had caused me nothing but grief. He was an adult, and I was not prepared to deal with any other person's mental health issues other than mine. Gary stayed a couple of weeks with me before leaving to go to visit his half-brother.

The man's mother continued to call me. She wanted me to be a part of their life. Once more, to not draw hard and fast lines I succumbed to playing nice which was a mistake. He didn't live in Roberta's trailer for very long but rented an apartment nearby in town near his mother. Calling me continually, I could tell someone had been at my house while I was at work, I began to think, although I didn't want to, there was no recourse other than obtaining an order of protection once more. Since he had worked at the Sheriff's Department as a dispatch operator, everyone there knew him. One instance when there had been nails scattered in the rear of my tires on my car that was sitting in my driveway, I called to report it to the police. Responding to the call no report was made of the incident, so there was no record of it. It was unrealistic the way things were managed.

There was a man at work by the name Sam who had given me his phone number on break one evening and asked me to call him. Waiting a couple weeks later to do it, one Sunday evening I called. We talked for hours. Seeming to be a nice person, I accepted an invitation to have a lunch date the following weekend. Not wanting anything more than friendship, I realized friendship with another is a complex issue with twists and turns unimaginable. More on this later. At the time it was a godsend in many ways. We began seeing one another daily. He would pick me up and drive me to work and we rode home together. We became a couple. One Friday evening after work we were sitting on my sofa watching television when there was a loud boom at my front door, the man who was stalking me had kicked it. Opening the door, he stepped into my living room. Yes, I had left the door unlocked. He proceeded toward me with his arms outstretched in a shooter's stance. Angered, I walked confidently toward him, he turned and fled. He was a coward and I'm glad he was. He very well could have been armed and dangerous. As it was, he was just dangerous. Being disrespected in my home simply because of cultural training, as well as at the urging of the person with me; caused me to decide to go downtown to the county seat and take an order of protection then and there. Stating the facts of what had happened that evening as well as the fact of other occurrences that had been going on, an order was issued. Satisfied I had done the right thing, I felt I had taken the only course of action I could take. After the summons had been served, I was notified by mail it had been done, along with a court date. Assuming the issue would be resolved, I felt more at ease. However, this was not to be the case.

Visiting Susan before work a day before the court date was scheduled, my cell phone rang. It was Sam, the man I was seeing at the time and the same person who had accompanied me to take the order of protection. He said, "I thought you said your court date was tomorrow". Replying, "I did, that is what my notification said". He said he had checked the court docket, and it was that very day at one o'clock. I was already dressed for work and had just enough time to make it downtown to attend the hearing. The man I had taken the order against was there, looking like a walking corpse. White faced and haggard, he stared at me when I walked in, and I had to step over his extended legs to reach a chair to sit down. Our case was called. The judge gave each of us a chance to speak. Without preamble, I stated all I wanted was the person to leave me alone. His turn came and he began an attempt to paint me as someone who had taken advantage of him but could not coherently explain in what manner. Saying I had hurt him, and he was fragile, the judge listened intently before asking him if he thought he could honor the order to stay away from my home? He said he could and that was the end of it. I went on to work. Not understanding why, I had been given a wrong court date initially, in retrospect it became clear that he had contacted people he had worked with, and they had done all they could to cause me to miss the date thereby causing a delay in the inevitable, because had I missed it, I would have promptly initiated another. The insaneness of the whole mess was a perfect example of small-town thinking along with gender entitlement. Having the history I had, it was not a manner of behavior I could accept. Thankful Sam had given me a "heads up" on the issue at hand.

Sam and I began seeing one another on a regular basis. Riding to work together and spending time at his apartment, I was living there for a while. He had taken me to meet his family. He had a daughter and granddaughter who lived with his parents. He had met my family. His affiliation with the opposite sex presented as if there was no special person in his life but we never discussed being exclusive. It seemed as if it was expected on my part, but not on his. Hesitation on how to continue and not understanding his entanglement with a woman and her daughter, he seemed to be at their beck and call, my interpretation was one of go on with my life, with him being an acquaintance to see occasionally. His demeanor changed toward me, and a sullenness ensued. Reminiscent of a teenager's behavior toward a parent. Wanting me to feel the same about these two women he was seeing, as he, which was feel sorry for their situation. Knowing all I knew about human nature, and the way he showed me he was, I knew if I said anything I would be labeled as jealous and I was not. It was simply that I saw through all the manipulations he wanted to talk to me about concerning them. For instance, when he said he was aggravated with the woman's daughter always calling him when she needed to go somewhere, and I suggested she could call Grits, which is a transportation system giving rides to people on state support, he got mad at me. Unable to do the battle a relationship would entail, time spent with him became nearly intolerable. Every encounter turned into his trying to pick a fight with me. Dealing with my life was all I could do, I could not manage another, causing me to distance myself from him. He had been married for many years, and it had been a typically structured relationship of male patriarchy, and my history was totally different. He wanted to present himself as an understanding person, but the culturally different subconsciousness became apparent in both of us, causing a disruption in the relationship. It seemed to be on one day, off the next and that was a rollercoaster I was not prepared to ride. Needing settledness only I could give myself, I saw no reason to continue. Coming from the background I had, I was dealing with my own mental state, with nothing to share with another person other than pleasantness. Both my grown children were attempting to find their place in the world and were continually in and out of my home, so navigating a personal relationship of understanding another was impossible for me at the time.

Life will take over matters, not the manufacturing process of one's own thinking, and the waves on the sea of life grew high. Work at the factory began to seem intolerable when we were put on ten hours a night. Unable to sleep. I would take lorazepam so it would knock me out for a few hours, only to wake again too soon without proper rest. The pain on the left side of my body became unbearable. Visiting my doctor, he told me it was probably psychosomatic, putting me on several different medications that didn't help at all. Researching the term, I told him surely, I did not hate myself as much as the pain I obviously was inflicting on myself. Accepting the fact that I could no longer maintain the work I was doing was a difficult realization. Requesting some time off, my doctor gave me the note needed to ensure I would not be terminated from employment. Contacting human resources, I set up a meeting to deliver the paperwork and talk with them about my short-term disability. Driving home from the meeting I had to pull over to the side of the road because the tears were coming so hard and fast, I could not see to drive. When I got home, I lay on the sofa attempting to relax, but my pain was so great in my left leg I decided it had to be cancer.

Sam came to visit me during this time and seemed to thrive on the personal problems I was having. Offering to take me to appointments in a neighboring town when I applied for my social security disability, since I was not familiar with the area. Accepting his offers since I had no other persons to rely on, I remained wary because I had seen his nature and unknown to him it sought to abase and demean the person I was. Not realizing the reasons I had stopped seeing him in the past, since I ignored the behavior exhibited, without telling him about it, my thinking was he should know, is the fault in my part in it continuing. An example of one aspect of his actions was he would visit before I went to work every day, bringing me coffee from McDonalds. When he complained that he had to wait a long time in the drive-through I said he shouldn't have waited, it made him angry. Another time I made some yellow squash fritters and was eating them while we were talking. He was sitting on a swivel rocker in my living room. I was sitting on my sofa. He turned the chair around and sat facing the wall, in a somewhat catatonic state. Unable to process the reason for this absurd behavior, I ignored it but decided I must distance myself from that type of energy, because I didn't understand it. Our relationship was not moving me forward nor was it feeding my soul.

I had bunions on my toes and had seen a podiatrist about having them removed. During this time Sam and I were not as involved as we had been. It seemed he was trying to be nicer, but the ugliness of cultural training continued raising its head. One of male dominance along with rigidity in thinking was hard to be around. Having to walk on eggshells to maintain any semblance of courtesy when I was more accustomed to openness and unwilling to conform to jumping through hoops to keep a person from fussing at me all the time was a price I was unwilling to pay. Owning my home, yet needing an income to maintain myself, I was totally unprepared mentally when after the surgery I was convalescing at Susan's house when I got a call on my cell phone. It was my son, calling to say he was on his way to see me. He arrived later that evening and we left Susans' and went back to my home. I had been away for a while and needed groceries. He was hungry, and drunk. There was some bread and cheese as well as some tomatoes I had saved from a plant Sam had put in the back yard that summer. Picking them green, wrapping them in newspaper and storing them in a Styrofoam cooler in the basement they were perfectly ripe, so he made himself a sandwich. I sat on the sofa drained of energy. Unable to walk because of the pin in my toe, using a crutch when I didn't want to wear the surgery boot which had to be fastened with Velcro fasteners and was a bitch to put on and take off, sometimes I would crawl on the floor to go to the bathroom or kitchen, or hop because it was easier. This was early November with Thanksgiving coming up I decided to cook dinner for my family and friends. Gary had gotten employment with a concrete contractor and was making good money, but he seemed to be incapable of making and sticking to any course of action concerning his life. He had married and they had twins that were two years old, so each weekend he went to get them and bring them to my house. That was fine with me but the yelling and screaming he would do with their mother was more than I could bear. One instance while they were on the phone I took his phone from his hand and hung it up, telling him that if they couldn't speak civilly to one another they had to stop talking. Giving the phone back to him, he promptly recalled her, and the tirade began all over again.

Visiting the doctors regularly I was sinking fast. My son coming was adding more stress and cost to my existence and there was no reaching him. Knowing there was no way to address any issues with him concerning his behavior I said nothing. He would visit his uncle in the neighboring county sometimes. Each time returning drunk. One such occasion he came into the house and accosted me with words unseemly for a son to address his mother with. All I did was look at him and say go to bed. He went to bed, but I was awake for the remainder of the night. Next morning he apologized to me. All I could manage was that's okay. Disheartened by the disrespect displayed, my mental state was at an all-time low. The doctor had prescribed a new antidepressant for me to take, Cymbalta. Beginning to take it, the first dose, it was all I could do to make it from the sink in the kitchen back to the sofa to sit down. Hindsight tells me there is no way it could have gotten in my system that quickly, yet I was overcome with dizziness to the point where I sat on the sofa the remainder of the day.

Sam happened to call. We had been estranged for a period, but with Gary coming back home, he had befriended him by calling to see if he could assist him in making a sidewalk at his parents' house. Gary did the job and that is how he integrated himself back into my life. We began seeing one another, he under the guise of seeing how I was doing. Coming for tea in the afternoon was okay at first. Leaving one day he tried to kiss me, and I turned my head. I did not want any intense involvement. Relationships with the opposite sex had proven to be more than I could navigate successfully. With their dominating nature and wanting their way on every front, caused me more grief than I cared to tolerate. Expectations of sex on demand, inconsiderate of weather you wanted it or not, irrespective of the circumstance was not appreciated and I saw no reason for such things. Risking an explosion of negative energy when refused and a sullenness of behavior, to me is not the way to entice another to want to lay down with you, let alone spread the legs. Again, my takeaway is one of this is not a positive way of being.

The day following Gary apologized to me. Sam visited me while Gary was at work. One look at my face and he knew something was wrong. "What happened?", he asked. Telling him about the altercation of the previous evening, he asked me a pivotal question.

"I'm looking at buying a house and I want you to come with me", he said. I answered, "okay". Without preamble, no terms on my part, nothing. My reptilian brain clicked in, I was fleeing a scene perceived as dangerous, seeking safety. Still not wanting a sexual relationship, he seemingly accepted it. At least on face value, I expected to be heard and respected by my words. This was not to be the case. I was a challenge to him to be conquered and overcome. As crazy as it sounds it is the truth. We went to look at the house. It was small, but new construction and nice enough. When Gary attempted to talk to me about the incident that was the precursor to my decision, which he knew nothing about, I simply said, "I don't want to talk about it, I know what I'm going to do". As hard as it was to make the decision, it had to be done because I could not stand emotionally to see my son wreck himself the way he was doing. Did I use Sam? Did Sam use me? Yes, and yes. Was it wrong? Who is to make a judgement call such as that? There is no such thing as a great love affair. Love is both a noun and a verb. It is intangible and as such impossible to process instantaneously. The manifestations of love are tangible, and this is what makes it so hard and easily abandoned by manmade ties. Blood ties between child and parent cannot be severed. The love is innate, yet the foisting onto another emotions only one can manage oneself is the hardest part of parenting. Moving from my home, I still was concerned about my son, yet the way he was behaving I could not live with. At the onset, Sam and I were okay, as time went on though, he began to exhibit behaviors showing me that my words had not been heard and would not be honored. Disallowing the creation of natural physical love to come about on its own, he began with demands. Expectation always precedes disappointment and is needed for disappointment to manifest. His needs were paramount to mine, and we could find no meeting of minds. It seemed he was engaged in payback where I was concerned. To show me how wrong I was by thinking I could have any feelings about how I wanted my life to go and have it go that way. So many opportunities are missed by this way of thinking. Since I was raised with the same mentality,

I understood it and was able to navigate, yet the underlying message was one of revenge and payback to me for being the way I am and creating myself the way I had. Consequently, sex became an act of more anger and defiance than love and respect. We were not on an even playing field and I knew it. I'm not sure if he was aware of what was going on or not, but I was fully aware of the dynamics and how to play to keep trouble down as much as possible. Trouble came each time we were around certain of my family members. My decision to keep trouble away from me caused it to follow me. Our saving grace was I had learned that fighting against a thing causes that thing to be bigger in one's life.

I had told Gary he could continue living in my house by paying me 300 dollars a month and the utilities. The utilities remained in my name, the responsibility was mine, so he didn't always pay them. He paid me 300 dollars one time. Coming to where Sam and I were living after work one Friday, he had the cash, and threw it on the counter in the kitchen with a sneer on his face. Not understanding his thinking as to the role, I was expected to play in his life, I was obviously not playing the role per his specifications. Such is the manipulative energy I was getting from my son. Sam and I went to visit my house on a regular basis. He worked part-time at the community center in town on weekends, so while he was at work, I would go to my house and hang out, or visit Susan, since she was within walking distance from my house. Gary had moved a woman and her two teenage children in with him, and this woman seemed to hate me. She resented me and blamed me for the way my son was toward her. He didn't treat her well, but he wasn't treating anyone in his life well, not even himself. Such is the manner of drug addicts. Neither of them was concerned with paying the rent, so the rent was not paid. I allowed this to continue for fifteen months. It seemed he was pushing me to see how far he could go and was surprised I allowed it to go on that long. Knowing something had to be done it took me two weeks to figure out an acceptable and fair way to tell them I had to regain my property. My notes on the decision are still in my journal entry from 2011. Deciding to offer to sell the house to them both or separately, the price I offered was below market value by at least ten thousand dollars. Concluding that a loss on the property was worth it to salvage my sanity and portrayal of the right thing to do.

It was on a Sunday when I went there to talk to them. She was lying on the sofa; the house was a mess. Walking in I had brought an overnight bag, with some clothing and towels in it to solidify the message that it was my house, and I could be there should I choose. Informing them we could not continue to do things as we had been doing, I needed to sell the house and was giving them first dibs. She told me she wasn't stable enough to buy a house, Gary got up and went outside. Neither one of them was interested in my offer. This was a difficult move for me to make but the way things were going something bad was going to happen there unless someone done something. I had realized this a few months prior which prompted my knowing that fact. Visiting one weekend I walked down to Susans for a visit. She and I walked back up to my house together to retrieve something I had given her. Garys girlfriend's son who was fourteen years old at the time was sitting on the front porch with a rifle laying across his knees and suddenly I had a premonition that he wasn't going to allow his mother to be treated the way she had been allowing herself to be treated. Gary was harassing her with words. Making fun of all of them. His behavior was fueled by alcohol and pills which the woman had told me she was addicted to. It was pure providence that brought me there that day. I truly believe that young man was planning to shoot my son. When Susan and I approached, the energy was something we both felt and agreed on when we left. The boy got up and left. She and I stayed long enough for the negativity to subside. Walking back down to her place we concurred on the thing we both had sensed. I'm so thankful it turned out as it did. Learning a valuable lesson I already knew, but needed to be reinforced, if a thing cannot continue, the sooner it is stopped the better. We all strive to make life better, easier and more productive for our offspring, but it is ultimately up to them to create the type of life they want for themselves, not us.

The evening after telling them I was taking back over; I was at home when my phone rang. It was Garys girlfriend. She wanted to know where he was, and did I know? I did not, but she didn't believe me. Worried about him, I had to keep my emotions under control because what I had done was the right thing to do, yet it was not without emotional pain attached. She had told me she was unable to find anywhere else to live and I was concerned about putting her out with children, but I could not be responsible for them. Staying away from the house for the remainder of the week, when I returned on Saturday, I didn't know what I would find. Thankfully she was gone. She had moved out.

Still not knowing where Gary was, as a mother I worried, yet had to continue with my life because I was still breathing. He had left his cell phone at the house, so I had no way to contact him. Suspecting he had returned to his wife; I had no way of knowing. He knew how to get in touch with me, so I accepted the fact that he didn't want to. Feeling scared for him there was nothing I could do.

I began once again cleaning up the mess he had left behind. So reminiscent of the thing we had been through a few years before with the biggest difference being there were small children involved now, who loved him as only children can love their father. The pain I felt for them was horrific. Estranged from them I was unable to enjoy their innocent sweetness and the exposure to the volatility of my son's personality caused visible upset in them, which was painful to see. It was as if he was thriving on the pain, he could cause others. His wife and he were not divorced at the time. He had returned to live with her and the children. Finding this out when he called, I was glad to know he was alive. Unconcerned as far as how he conducted his life and affairs, I just wanted to know he was alive and well. My punishment was not over yet though. Somehow, he had it in his mind I was able to pay his way. Calling me on a Saturday to see if I would pay the rent on an apartment he and she had rented, I refused. It wasn't right and I could not see fit to do it. Crying, he hung up on me. Feeling badly for his mental state, yet realizing his thinking was remiss, I had to maintain myself for myself. Later that evening my phone rang, and it was his wife telling me he had run his car into a telephone pole and had been airlifted to a hospital in Little Rock. This news drained me of all my strength and courage. Unable to go to the hospital because I couldn't stand to see him in that state, I called Emma, told her the news, and she and her husband went there. Life at this time was nearly unbearable. My pain was immense. There was nothing I could do, still breathing so I was alive, that's about it. Getting through the next few weeks I functioned on habits I had always used to see me through. Eating healthily, exercise and not talking about what was going on. I somehow knew it would get over with, I just didn't know how. Once he got out of the hospital, I went to see him at the apartment where they lived. He had broken his neck, and the convalescent period was quite a while. He couldn't work, so once more I was called on to pay their rent. His paybacks were harsh, but not nearly as harsh as the price the twins had to pay. This brought home the saying that it's the children who suffer the most. Extrication from this mess was proving to be a difficult process. Having no diagram to assist me in navigating the scenario, I proceeded on. It seemed like a battle of wills I was engaged in without my assenting to it. His attempts to make me pay his way seemed non-ending. It would be easy to pass judgment, but I cannot conceive anyone wanting to cause that much harm unless they were suffering an intense pain manifesting into actions such as the ones he was displaying. Therefore, I could not judge, only pray for some clarification for him and myself as well. Attempts to control another person can never cause anything good to happen. Intention of the heart will come about but much suffering will precede the intent, and self-destructive habits do not speed up the process of healing. They very well may end the life of the individual either inadvertently or on purpose. The accident in no way do I think was planned, but the magnitude of where he found himself in a position of responsibility, he was not prepared to manage, became overwhelming. We've all been there in one way or another and remaining in the present is the antidote, however we sometimes cannot do it, especially when we begin drawing lines and creating blame. Neither he nor his wife were in the marriage for the right reasons. I had no part to play yet was being instigated in a situation where I was in the role without the script, thus I had to remove myself and did.

Preceding my moving in with Sam, my doctor had prescribed several medications for me to take, to ease the transition of retirement. These pills were deadening my senses, which needed deadening since I was feeling too much and couldn't do anything about what was going on in the lives of my children as well as myself. Being vulnerable, I was ill prepared to begin a romantic relationship as Sam wanted and he was ill prepared to accept me as I was. Even after using my words the best way I knew how, to convey this message to him, his comprehension was remiss to the point of believing his thoughts rather than my words. Such is the manner we as humans tend to revert to when faced with challenges unfamiliar to us. Teachings from our earliest years, mimicking the actions we have observed in our authority figures, rather than listening to the people in our life as humans stating their needs, we act out genders. We all do this to some extent, and that is why things can begin looking the same, no matter the circumstance. Comparison and expectations color our behavior, with blame and clear-cut lines drawn inviting more of the same, even though situations and people are so different. This is the best explanation I can come up with as to what ensued following our moving in together. Knowing his way of thinking came easier to me than mine came to him. His thoughts seemed to be that I was taking advantage of him and his resources, even though we alternated paying for groceries when we went to the store. He continued to work at various jobs. He had quit the job at the community center and started working at a hardware store. We played house, with me staying home doing the housework, cooking, cleaning and such. He did the yardwork on his off days and continued taking care of his parents outside work at their house. We went there and I hung out with them or assisted him with whatever he was doing such as painting or sweeping the sidewalk and porch after he cut the grass. His demeanor toward me was alternating between harshness and criticism. Not knowing what to make of it, I remained quiet because I knew I wasn't doing anything to warrant such energy coming my way. Argument was not in my realm of comprehension; I could see no reason for it. Allowing him to speak to me in whatever way he chose, since I had sold my house, I had no choice of anywhere to go. My income was limited, with housing prices having accelerated to the point I could not afford to purchase anything comparable to what I'd had, it was a hard spot for me to realize myself being. His attitude toward women was becoming more and more apparent and I could not do combat with a thing I had no control over, which was ingrained teachings. My saving grace and his was the fact we had no one else in our lives to turn to. What I was faced with was the culture I had been raised in and sought to flee, had fled, and returned to. Whatever part I was playing was foreign to me. Once more I was lost in the onslaught of life. We weren't on the same page at all. His comparisons of me and my children were based on the views prevalent in our society and I had a different experience having the history of being a single parent as well as several marriages and a business owner, the situation was recognizable but unacceptable. Not knowing how to respond, my communication was minimal, sparse and prethought to avoid upsetting him. His fits and accusations were unfounded so there was no way to connect. Sex was perfunctory on my part and demanded on his part. Both of us were miserable; the difference being I could make no accusations because I knew he couldn't help it, somehow it seemed he had to get rid of his energy in a negative accusatory way onto me. Dominance was the order of the day. Knowing this was not what he wanted, I knew it wasn't what I wanted, so I set about injecting any truth I could muster in any way I could at any time I could. Forcing me to rise above and transcend this existence to a higher level even as I had done in my past.

Sam and I both were struggling. His words were his unfiltered thoughts. I had sold my Honda Accord to Emma, so I had no vehicle, dependent on him for housing and getting around, it became unbearable to be in the car with him for any period, because I was a captive audience and had to listen to whatever words were chosen. Thankfully for us both I had enough life "under my belt" to realize the words were not reflective of me nor my presentation of the life I wanted to create. Beginning to look for housing he said he wanted to assist me in finding something suitable. Looking at various properties in the city, he found fault with everything we looked at. Prices were out of my range since I had retired and was living on Social Security, the properties we looked at were much less attractive than the house I had sold. He continued to want to have sex with me, telling me that my skin crawled when he touched me, which was a misconception on his part because I was numb to anything remotely associated with feeding or detracting from the male ego. My need for self-compassion was demanding all my focus. Not understanding the situation, I found myself in, I'm sure he felt the same way. Neither of us were prepared to live this existence we had created. Not knowing where to start, I began firstly, ridding myself of the pills the doctors kept prescribing for me. Developing a rash on my upper chest and neck area, it was a burning/itching sensation I managed to live with by using cortisone cream and wearing only one hundred percent cotton tops. Suspecting it was a reaction to something I was taking, I asked the doctor if it could be that. He said it wasn't. By this time, I was taking seven different pills. Seeking a second opinion I sought help from a therapist. After our first meeting when I told her I wanted help getting off all the pills I was taking, she talked with me for an hour, then wrote me a prescription, saying she was having good results with a new drug, Celexa. Dumfounded by her lack of hearing what I had asked for, I took the prescription, walked out of her office, threw it in the garbage can in the reception area, and left. Realizing I was on my own attaining the thing I needed. There was no understanding to be had, writing in my journal, "I cannot even buy a friend", since I had to pay her. Seeking help with the skin problem I visited a dermatologist. She didn't work at the office I was seen at but was temporarily assigned, filling in three days a week in the office I was seen since they had no staff dermatologist at the time. Thankfully she was compassionate and listened to my concerns. I had begun cutting down on the pills but was still taking Cymbalta, and I thought it was an allergic reaction to that, even though I had been assured it was not. When I told her my suspicions, she agreed that was exactly what it was. She said she had seen it before, it would take anywhere from nine months to a year for it to resolve. Warnings on such meds say not to stop taking them "cold turkey", so Sam got me some empty capsules so I could cut the dosage down incrementally. Beginning to do that, I had researched how to get off these types of drugs, it said talk to everyone in your life that you had a relationship with daily. Tell them you might have moods swings resulting in being short with them in communication, as well as other matters, such as being less tolerant than usual. At this time, I was speaking to one of my sisters daily and she was not the easiest person to talk to. She took antipsychotic meds to manage her thinking, so she could be challenging at times to talk with. When I told her my plans to stop all the pills, and try to overlook any shortcomings I might display, she said she understood, as did Sam, with his words. Seemingly condescending and sympathetic, he did not know how to receive my request without coloring it with pity. The first time I replied with a less than acceptable manner in his way of thinking he went off on me. He was not used to me being any way other than quiet and responding to him without anything other than acceptance. Quieting me momentarily there were issues in our relationship needing addressing and I had allowed things to get so out of alignment I knew I had to say something whether I wanted to or not, and I did not, knowing the fight I would have on my hands. Firstly, it seemed to not be understood that I did not like him talking adversely about my family. My siblings were people I loved, it hurt to have them denigrated. As the old saying goes, "I can talk about my family members but no one else can". It seemed these things did not matter to him. Knowing that it would not improve anything by doing to him what he was doing to me, I decided the next time it happened I would simply say, "don't do that". It so happened he was at work on this particular day, and it was on my mind so heavily because of comments made in an earlier conversation. I knew he didn't like certain members of my family and made no attempt to understand that I loved them and how it made me feel to hear them talked about in a judgmental manner. Discounting it as cultural, as I knew it was, it was one of the traits I had fled from in my youth. Sending him a Marco Polo, I stated do not talk about my family members to me anymore. Stated just that simply. Knowing there would be a backlash; I went to bed but couldn't sleep. He got home at ten thirty at night, and I heard him unlock the door. Getting up, I ventured down the hallway to take whatever he was ready to put on me. As I knew it would be, he immediately tore into me with verbiage that I was never to say anything like that to him ever again. Having told him once before not to do it, face to face, was the reason I sent a Marco Polo that time. The first time he had held up the middle fingers on both hands and said, "I'll say anything about anybody anytime". I could not abide an onslaught like that again, but the talk had to stop. How we managed to get past this way of doing is beyond me. I didn't want to hear it, I cannot imagine him wanting to say it, but it was happening and seemed to be taking on a life of its own. The other thing to confront was the way he viewed my children. It seemed to me that he was ill prepared to accept they existed. They did exist and the "water to be trod" to cause an understanding of my unconditional love for them seemed unable for him to comprehend. Since this is such volatile territory, dealing with perceived indiscretions on their part, I knew my words must be thought out rather than approached mindlessly. Mindlessness is the cause of most all emotional upset between people. Remaining calm and assessing the situation from a neutral perspective along with knowing presentation of less than stellar attributes is a signpost of the presenters' experience, rather than a signal to behave and believe in the same manner as them. Learning this is valuable yet hard to incorporate knowledge. Lifelong exposure to different ways of thinking and being, not accepting rather allowing others to be the way they are is the only way to progress. Not attacking rather watching and allowing. Some things naturally affect us more than others. Competition and comparison have no place in mutually caring relationships. Yet it is there; and without carefully handling these emotions they can successfully ruin something that had the potential to be beautiful yet turned ugly in an instant. Indiscretions of all manner were occurring on every turn. Watching this was sort of like watching a movie. Once more I was playing a part in a show, I had no script to follow. Such is the beauty of life, relying on understanding of the ill's others will foster onto and potentially in us are really the manifestations of their own perception, yet the onslaught of controlling behavior cannot be dismissed. Strong personal assessment, accountability and acceptance of oneself is emphasized and realized when accosted with these things. Self-realization and actualization rise to the surface when we can admit to ourselves the validity of whether the life, we are creating is one we can abide and flourish in or change the things needing changing. Demanding scrutiny of self without any judgement of anyone or anything. Thinking another should know something they are clearly showing they do not know demands we tell them. If they cannot accept that or show uncaring about our feelings, we must believe that as well and create whatever the acceptance and allowing their way of being, to be. We oversee nothing but ourselves.

Applying for senior housing in a development of apartments that had been built in the vicinity where we lived, we looked at them when they first opened. They were nice. Two-bedroom units, small but acceptable. The wait list was two years, so I stayed put in the place where we lived. It was small as well. Initially both our names were on the deed and mortgage, but I had signed a quit claim at one point in our relationship when he had run both me and my daughter off when she had come for a short visit. The climate in the house was tense from the get-go since she was having some domestic difficulties in her marriage, and it was reflected in her aura. Sam had taken it upon himself to straighten her out. I was still a smoker at the time, so I had gone to the garage to smoke. It was early morning and we all had just gotten up. Hearing voices as I sat smoking, I smiled inside because I thought they were talking to my grandson who was a baby at the time. Ashing out my cigarette, I entered the kitchen from the garage. With a smile in my heart, I walked inside. The voices were not of the thing I had imagined. Sam was in my daughters' face screaming that she was a the lowest of the low. Frozen in place, I stood in the kitchen and allowed the drama to play out in front of me. Not knowing what to do I done nothing. She had her phone in her hand, had dialed 911, and Sam took off into the bedroom muttering obscenities under his breath. I went to him, he was hurriedly dressing saying he was leaving, then I went to her. The police had called back since she had hung up on them. Assuring them all was well and under control, she and I hurriedly packed up her things and carried them to her vehicle. Walking out with her, we both were near tears, but I was past tears, because I had seen this coming for a while. Both had been stewing for an altercation. Her visit was to be for three days, so my stance was knowing she would be leaving so her mood was a thing I could tolerate, whereby he felt she was acting in an insubordinate manner.

Once she was gone, his tirade against me continued. Talking nonstop about her, calling her vile unseemly names, I dared not counter. Attempting to calm him, I gave him a lorazepam. Yes, I could see where he was coming from, but it was he and I who were in a relationship together, not she and him. She was going through a difficult period at that time. Being a new mother is not an easy thing, and the misunderstanding was great. Unable to use my words to explain anything to him without causing further chagrin, I said nothing. Again, culture traditions were causing a rift in understanding, manifesting to a separation that was unavoidable.

Next morning, using Sam's car, I went to the grocery store wanting to continue with life as we knew it. He was not ready to let it go though. His attack continued and became an attack on me. Making lunch, attempting small talk, he was not able to talk about anything else other than my daughter. This way of being continued for days. Berating and demeaning it was more than I could tolerate. Neither of them was aware of me having any feelings at all. She had been acting in an aversive manner for a long time toward me. I saw it but I knew who I was, I was the parent, she was the child acting in a childish way. Ignoring rather than calling it out since it was something she had to work out with herself. It was irrelevant to me since I was at peace with my principles as a parent. The only thing left for me now was making a livable life for myself and Sam's behavior was challenging me in that respect.

Since I didn't have a car, I called a car dealership and ordered a Honda Civic by phone. They brought it to me that day. Sitting at the table in the kitchen with the salesperson, I wrote him a check-in full for the purchase price. Sam stayed in the living room. He seemed to be observing me, my actions, and not understanding why I would not fight with him.

I was at my wits end. Having heard this statement many times I truly found the meaning of it. Being in a spot I seemingly had negated years prior, obviously there were still lessons to be learned I had missed. Knowing the way things were going yet still wanting to maintain peace, I realized that I had to leave Sam, even though I didn't want to. Since I had moved in with him, we had constructed a conventional living situation, dictated by the conventions of societal rules we both had been raised with, consequently it seemed the disrespect manifested was intuitive of the male domination I had abhorred as a child, along with a feeling of not recognizing myself. By listening to the abasement coming my way I was moved to quit the arrangement and having nowhere to go I, I packed all my belongings in the back of my car and drove to where my son was living with his wife. She had rented a three-bedroom house. Never unpacking, I spent some time with them before going on to where my daughter lived. Still no unpacking was done. Living out of my car, I did put in a change of address and filled out an application for senior housing, which was about twenty minutes from her house. Being this unsettled after the life I had lived up to this point was somewhat humiliating and disconcerting to my psychic. Unable to dissect the meaning of all I had experienced in my relationship with Sam, I continued to wonder what feeling of power he garnered by behaving to me the way he did. It was reminiscent of the way I had treated Duncan when we first began seeing one another. Further garnering my understanding of human nature. Seeing the manifestation of living an existence created from less than desirable behaviors.

It was winter by this time and having been at Emma's home for a few months, it was snowing. She was cooking supper, and it was plain she was having some tension toward me. I felt it. Without preamble, I knew it was time to leave. My existence was in such turmoil I was unable to traverse the territory of toleration required to ride this wave. Getting up from playing with my grandson I gathered my personal items and simply walked out the door. Driving to Holiday Inn Express, I phoned Sam on the way. He was ecstatic to hear from me, feeling as if he had won a battle, which I never understood in the first place. Returning to what was now his house since I had signed a quit claim deed. Things continued to be the same as they had been before, prompting me to be more conscious of setting boundaries with the least said possible. I did understand where he was emotionally, but I had already traveled the road he was on and knew it led to nowhere except division and disunity. There had to be another way and I was adamant to find it. Each time he displayed the antics he had presented in the past, not wanting to, I calmly confronted them. Googling the issue of stopping up his ears while I ate, it said there was a mental condition called misophonia which is described as selective sound sensitivity syndrome. After sharing this with him it became easier to accept. He had been attempting to blame me, saying it was the way I was raised in an uncouth manner causing me to bang my spoon on my plate, bowl or whatever I was eating from. As far as the demeaning way he spoke about my family members was concerned, that took much longer. Not demanding any change in his thinking, because it is on everyone how they process their private thoughts, expressing them as truth is a falseness I am ill prepared to accept.

Upon returning I insisted on having my name reinstated on the deed and mortgage to insure having a place to live. Deciding if he wanted to fight, it would not be foisted on me. Each attack was responded to rather than reacted to. Learning much useful information and acceptance about myself, Sam began an attempt to learn how to love me better in a way I could accept. Deciding we needed a bigger house we began the process of looking for a better more accommodating place to live. During the move things did not go well. The place was for sale by the owner. We made an offer, it was accepted, the deal was closed, we got the key, but the person would not move. Giving the man another week, I had to pay the person who bought our house a hundred fifty-eight dollars, so we could stay there another week. Contacting the man we bought from, he was evasive about when he would move, saying he would reimburse me the money, he made no move to do so. Attempting to talk to him the Sunday before the bought week began, he walked away from us mid conversation. I told Sam we were going to have to put him out because we had to move. Selling our house, we were now renting it for one hundred fifty-eight dollars a week. Sam felt unsure about doing it, even though I knew it was okay, he wanted to go talk to the county attorney. That Monday we went downtown and spoke with the county attorney. He said, "it's your house, what's the problem?" "Change the locks and take possession of it". Contacting a locksmith to meet us at the house, we had the locks changed. Calling the man at work, I told him, "We are taking possession of our house, I would suggest you come get your things if you want them". "They will be moved to the yard after which Salvation Army will be called to remove them from there". He said, "Kaye, what do you want me to do?" I said, "if I were you, I would leave work right now, rent a U-Haul and come get the things from the yard", which is what he done. When he walked down the gangplank from the rear of the truck, he looked dejected, and I truly felt sympathetic toward him, but it had to be done. Meanwhile many of his family members had come to assist him, so I had to summon the police because Sam was losing it. He became combative toward one of the women when they began taking down curtains that were supposed to stay. Police came. Asking who was the owner, we stated we were. Looking at the deed and our move in date which was a week prior to the present date, they maintained a presence until he got things loaded and was gone. It was once more embarrassing for me to have to assert myself the way I did.

Once we were moved, there were things needing to be done, such as the patio door replacement as well as painting and things of that nature. Sam was still working part-time, so it fell on me to do these things, which I did. The first year we lived there he went into a deep depression. It was a growing time for us both. Knowing I could not live in the environment that had been, I think he realized the same. At one-point things were so bad I called the bank to see if I could buy him out on the house. Since my income was not enough to do so, he seemed satisfied with the way things were, making no move to buy me out. With the battle continuing once more I was not able to participate. I was not savvy enough to see the point in fighting and didn't want that type of relationship. He would ask me to stay yet make it unpalatable to do so. Not seeming to understand how we needed to be with one another, it seemed everything was scripted. I became able to nearly know verbatim what words were going to be used and what tone was going to be set around any issue that arose. There was no creativity in life creation only a mindset of one-way thinking. Feeling smothered, my salvation was my journaling and meditation. Occasionally visiting my daughter for a few weeks, my son had become estranged from me, and I was alone.

My niece lived nearby so my weekly visits with her were sustaining, and I shared what I could with Sam to initiate some manner of relationship growth and acceptance. Acceptance of me as a person, not an inferior usable object. Continuing the duties of home maintenance, it was clear to me he was miserable. At one point his verbalizing of his thoughts were, I could give you forty thousand dollars. Without responding to the statement, I allowed it to fall on deaf ears because I didn't know how to respond. Knowing I had done nothing wrong, and his mindset reflected the ambiguity he was feeling. If we were to discuss a separation the time to discuss it was not the time he made the statement. His thoughts concerning the female species was reflected and interpreted by me as simply a receptacle of sperm, not an equal and capable fully rounded individual. All I was doing battle with was the specter of the reality I was raised with and the past relationships I had been in. My business demanded I not allow the mindset to affect me, yet in my real life I had to be accepted as the whole person I was and am. Capable, sure and able to take on anything that comes my way. That is how I choose to see myself. Lacking the capacity to internalize the negativity coming my way, I began devising an escape. Each time I applied to senior housing in the past and was called with a unit ready for me, he would ask me to stay, and I would. Then when the ugly demon emerged, I would be doubly angry with myself. Using the guise of joking, when he said I couldn't make it without him, I had to explain to him with a joke everyone laughed not just the one making the joke. For instance, he told me at one point that without him I would be homeless. That statement prompted me to get a job. Taking a part time seasonal position at a department store during the Christmas season was something I didn't like nor enjoy. The following spring I applied for and was hired to work at a long-term care facility, in the memory care unit. Working and caring for elderly people with Alzheimer disease. It was an easy job, and they were a joy to care for. Such fun we had, and things at home did get better. Somehow, I knew the things Sam had presented to me were not indicative of the life he wanted to live; it was just that he didn't know any better. Reflective of his upbringing, and mine, I had fled the scene and he had not. He stayed and was entrenched in the thinking that so many people buy into and honor, which is loving someone and having a life with them requires it be painful and full of strife, with one person dominating the environment, right or wrong. Going along with him if I could, it became intolerable and that is why the dynamics had to change. Knowing I needed to make more money than the income I had from Social Security, this job afforded me the opportunity to speak more freely, allowing myself to be known as the person I am, not a clone of an outdated era. It was three months into my employment when news came of my one of my elderly sisters impending death. She had an enlarged esophagus and when they attempted to stretch it the treatment didn't work. Giving her the option of intravenous feeding to stay alive or the consequences of transcending this existence to enter the next one. She opted for the latter. My niece and I decided to travel to her home to say our last goodbyes. The morning we went, I had worked the previous evening and awoke with a soreness in my neck and shoulder area. Thinking it was allergies because I had a slight congestion as well. Picking her up we journeyed to say goodbye. My niece was recovering from lymphoma and was in a weakened state. Covid had just hit the year before, and we had been sequestered for a long time. It felt good to have freer movement. Since we had been inoculated against it, we thought we were safe. She had been going to church again and I was working three days a week at my job. We made our goodbyes. Since there were several people there, she wore a mask, but while we were driving there, we didn't mask up. The drive was the better part of an hour, so with the windows up and the air conditioning running it was a closed environment in the vehicle. I don't know who infected who or where either of us was exposed, but we both came down with covid at the same time. Sam consequently got sick as well. My niece had to be hospitalized for 51 days due to complications associated with her compromised immune system. Keeping track in my journal of the duration and progress of the virus, I was sick twenty days. There was a couple of days when I felt as if death would be welcome over the way I was feeling. Sam was sick, though not as sick as I was. He spent two days in bed while I was in bed eight days, causing me to develop pneumonia. He was able to go to the store and buy soup for us to eat, which is what we subsisted on. Losing eight pounds during the ordeal, I finally started to feel better after getting antibiotics and steroids to combat the pneumonia in my lungs. Sam received no treatment and even mowed the grass once during his sickness. Losing six close family members to the virus it took many people in the swath it cut through our society. Hitting some harder than others. During the convalescent period I made some major decisions about my life. Telling Sam I would talk to him when I got better, when the time came for me to return to work, I decided to quit. My reasons for working were not for the money, rather for therapy for myself to regain some measure of self. Having lost so much from accommodating others, I had lost my own identity. Putting up with demeaning treatment from others in my immediate association to the point of them discounting me because I was discounting myself. By allowing my self-worth to emanate from outside myself, others' insecurities were foisted on to me and I embraced them as my own. Facing one's own fear of lack will bring experiences less than our best creation, causing one to lose oneself in the fray. Coming as near death as I did with covid, my decision to use my knowledge to create a better life for me was the positive take away from the negative experience, causing a breakthrough of sorts that was sorely needed.

Processing the position I was in and the courage it took to confront all that needed to be confronted, required I do extreme self-evaluation prompting me to write this my feeble attempt to understand the whys and wherefores of my existence and find an internal acceptance of me, without engaging in battles presented to me by the ones drawing lines, creating dissension and trying to abase and demean my existence to a level less than what I believe is our purpose when we inhale our first breath, taking us to our last exhalation. There is no promise of anything other than the honor we muster for ourselves, sans resistance to powers greater than all. Nature rules and going against it will ensure a less than stellar existence until finally she shows herself in her full glory. Borrowing a quote from Ralph Waldo Emerson, "every spirit builds itself a house; and beyond its house a world; and beyond its world, a heaven. Know then that the world exists for you. For you is the phenomenon perfect. What we are, that only we can see. All Adam had, all that Caesar could, you have and can do. Adam called his house heaven and earth; Caesar called his house, Rome; you perhaps call yours a cobbler's trade; a hundred acres of ploughed land; or a scholar's garret. Yet line for line and point for point, your dominion is as great as theirs, though without fine names. Build therefore your own world.

Coming to the end of this weaving together of words into the story of my progress to this point of my existence, it becomes clearer to me all the time that any hardships we endure is a tuning of the spirit to be known, along with the creation of a life suitable for inhabitation according to our personal beliefs. Anything other than is a travesty and sin against self. My wish and prayer is for all of humanity to exist in peace, acceptance, understanding, forgiveness and open honest communication. This alone will ensure the progress sorely needed for the advancement of us all.

Printed in the United States
by Baker & Taylor Publisher Services